INTRODUCTION

In 1984, a wiry Scotsman powered his way into Tour de France folklore by winning the iconic King of the Mountains polka dot jersey, finishing ahead of luminaries such as Laurent Fignon, Pedro Delgado and Luis Herrera. Along the way, he won the 11th stage of the Tour in the mountainous region between Pau and Guzet-Neige, turning in a spirited ascent of the iconic Alpe d'Huez and dropping the legendary Bernard Hinault on his way to the summit. As is reported in the biography, *In Search of Robert Millar*, Robert Millar first honed his skills on the many hillclimbs that were within easy reach of his home city of Glasgow. True, southern Scotland cannot offer the road cyclist such epic climbs as those of the Tour de France, the Giro d'Italia or the Vuelta a España, but it does provide a tremendous range of hillclimb challenges.

Many of southern Scotland's hillclimbs are already well known to Scotland's cycling club fraternity and are used regularly in cycling club training runs and confined events. The autumn season of competitive hillclimbing has brought riders to Dalry Moor (Scottish championships) and High Auldgirth (South West Scotland championships) in recent years. Longer road Time Trial classics have familiarised

many with the Crow Road (near the Campsies) and the Duke's Pass (Tour of Trossachs). Those favouring the Cyclosportive format for their timed rides are likely to have confronted the challenges of the Granites (Bethany Edinburgh Sportive), Burrowstown Moss (Ken Laidlaw Scottish Borders Sportive) and Talla Linn (Tour of Tweeddale Sportive).

Pro-cycling has also faced up to the hillclimbs of southern Scotland. The Tour of Britain challenged competitors to summit the Mennock Pass in both 2007 and 2008. The now defunct Girvan Cycle Race familiarised cyclists throughout Scotland with Nick o' the Balloch, Garleffin and many more climbs in South Ayrshire. Its successor, the Tour DoonHame, is making the most of what Dumfries & Galloway has to offer the road hillclimber.

Away from the cut and thrust of racing, Carrick Hill (National Route 7) and Pease Bay (National Route 76) may be familiar to cycle tourists who have used the Sustrans National Cycle Network. And yet, there are many more classic hillclimbs in southern Scotland that are little more than well-kept local secrets.

A small minority of cycle tourists actually enjoy hillclimbing, slipping into the 'granny gear' and effortlessly spinning their way to the top of the hill while enjoying the scenery. However, for the vast majority, the pleasure of hillclimbing rests in its physical challenge, the sense of achievement on reaching the crest of the hill and, of course, the reward of the downhill that lies over the horizon.

Despite our role models, our classic routes and the rewards we derive from it, road hillclimbing does not have a large following in Scotland. Perhaps the allure of mountain biking draws hillclimb-loving cyclists away, or maybe the renaissance of British track cycling has tempted cyclists away from the hills altogether. Then again, perhaps we need to celebrate road hillclimbing in Scotland and to signpost cyclists to the many opportunities on our doorstep. This book rises to the challenge.

Climb like a mountain goat

If you have already experienced the pleasure and pain of road hillclimbing, you'll know that it is a skill that can be developed with practice. What follows is some advice for cyclists of all abilities – helping you enjoy the climbs more by spending less time on them!

10 elementary tips for climbing

- Know the hill and plan the ascent in advance.
- Maintain momentum on approach to the climb, while avoiding the inclination to speed up. Speeding up on approach is more likely to result in burn-out than a quicker ascent.
- Know your gears, and how and when to use them effectively. When climbing, you will be using lower than normal gears.
- Gradually shift gears downwards on the ascent.
- Anticipate shifting gear and change before you have to. Shift down when you feel that your pedals are not spinning freely.
- Keep upright in your saddle – in direct contrast to the flats (and the descents), more power is available on the climb when you are in an upright position.
- Stand when you need extra power that cannot be met by shifting down gears (remembering that cycling out of the saddle burns more energy and should, therefore, be used selectively).
- Never get too tired or too hungry on the ascent – refuel and replenish depleted energy levels.
- If the climb is too taxing to be ascended without stopping, then aim to stop where you are afforded some shade and shelter (under trees, buildings, etc.).
- Invest in toe-clips (or preferably clip-in pedals) as this allows you to concentrate on pulling-up in your pedal rotations – this is the most efficient way to cycle, as gravity takes care of the downstroke.

10 tips to refine good climbing practice

- Try and keep your shoulders back (open) as this will improve oxygen intake.

THE CYCLIST'S GUIDE TO HILLCLIMBS ON
SCOTTISH LOWLAND ROADS

The author and publisher have made every effort to ensure that the information in this publication is accurate, and accept no responsibility whatsoever for any loss, injury or inconvenience experienced by any person or persons whilst using this book.

Dedication
To all my boyhood friends who accompanied me on our forays along country roads to far-flung parts of Ayrshire. In particular, I dedicate this to David Mason, my companion on a cherished teenage cycle/hiking expedition to Fort William. Rest in peace.

published by
pocket mountains ltd
Jenny Wren, Holm Street, Moffat DG10 9EB
www.pocketmountains.com

ISBN: 978-1-907025-25-9

Text copyright © John H McKendrick 2011
Photography copyright © John H McKendrick unless stated otherwise

The right of John H McKendrick to be identified as the Author of this work has been asserted by him in accordance with the Copyright, Designs and Patents Act 1988

A catalogue record for this book is available from the British Library

All route maps are based on 1945 Popular Edition Ordnance Survey material and revised from field surveys by Pocket Mountains Ltd, 2011. © Pocket Mountains Ltd 20011.

Printed in Poland

- A wider grip on the handlebars will help reduce breathing restriction (also making it easier to keep your shoulders open).
- Using lower gears with a greater number of pedal repetitions per minute (higher cadence) will place less strain on your knees than using higher gears with a lower number of pedal repetitions per minute (lower cadence). Aim for around 70 to 80 repetitions per minute for greatest efficiency.
- Stand up momentarily on less taxing parts of the climb to use different muscle groups and to stretch your back. This is particularly important on longer climbs.
- Only come out of the saddle in the steepest sections if you are sure that you will be able to stay out of the saddle until the gradient eases.
- Only come out of the saddle when you are in the right gear for that part of the climb – it is difficult to shift gear when standing.
- Get ready to come out of the saddle when one leg is at the top of the pedal stroke – as you push down on the pedal, pull yourself out of the saddle.
- Look ahead and keep elbows slightly bent when out of the saddle to maintain good posture and strong breathing.
- Practise – through time, knowing when to shift gear, when to come out of the saddle and when to push hard will become second nature. In particular, practise standing techniques on flats or shallow slopes.

- Develop your strength – on the hill, or in the gym. Upper body strength and a strong core should not be overlooked – climbing needs more than strong legs.

10 final tips towards perfecting hillclimbing technique

- Lose weight! Climbing is a power-to weight-activity – world-class climbers tend to be slightly built. Of course, there are exceptions (Miguel Indurain immediately springs to mind). The basic rule is that the lighter cyclist does not need to generate as much power as the heavier cyclist as he or she has less weight to carry uphill. Weight loss can also take the form of reducing bike weight. This might be a more palatable solution to maximising performance – do you really need that third water bottle?
- The main focus should be on improving climbing technique, rather than developing power through punishing hill repetitions.
- For extra power without standing or changing down gears, pull on the handlebars, as this allows you to follow on by pushing harder on the pedals.
- When standing, push your knees forward toward the handlebars, as this will help you gain extra power on your upstroke.
- Try and shift up gears the moment before you stand and shift down gears when you return to a sitting position – this will help you to maintain a steady momentum.

- Ride straight on all but the most severe inclines, as momentum, speed and energy will be lost weaving up the road.
- Have some really low gears on your bike to assist with longer and steeper climbs.
- Develop a regular pattern of breathing for greatest efficiency; for example by co-ordinating breathing with your pedal strokes.
- Visualise the climb and anticipate reaching the top at your planned speed.
- Divide the climb into distinct sections and coax yourself through each section, focusing on the immediate challenge (while leaving aside enough energy to complete the whole climb).

Descend like a rolling stone

This guide describes the ascent of some of southern Scotland's best road hillclimbs. Descents are not described, though, of course, working through the notes in reverse offers some advance warning of what lies ahead. There are two challenges to overcome in descent – fighting the wind and overcoming fear of speed.

10 top tips to get you started

- As for ascending, know the hill and plan the descent in advance.
- Ensure that your bike is in good condition – in particular, that both brakes are in good working order.
- Before descending, add layers at the summit to protect yourself from the wind-chill that your descent will generate.

- Brake gently and gradually, as required.
- Be aware that braking distances are greater when the road is wet.
- Brakes on a bike are not as good as those on a car, so don't get too close behind cars on the descent.
- Keep alert – constantly look ahead for gravel and potholes.
- Always be prepared to stop if going around a blind bend.
- Resist the urge to put your foot out for stability – it is more likely to throw you off balance and lead to a crash.
- Descend within your comfort zone – an anxious mind is not well-placed to respond to unforeseen dangers ahead.

10 tips to take you down faster

- Think positive. Remind yourself that you are in control. Do not focus on hazards. Instead, focus on how you will manage each hazard.
- Where the profile of the descent allows, accelerate to a high speed at the start of the descent.
- On reaching near maximum speed, tuck in and let gravity do its work.
- Pedal periodically on longer downhills to prevent the build-up of lactic acid in your leg muscles and to maintain maximum speed.
- Move your weight toward the back of your saddle. Bend elbows and knees, and relax, to absorb vibrations caused by rough surfaces.
- Look as far ahead as possible to make

timely adjustments in advance.

- When going around tight bends, drive down your outside leg, lean on your inside leg (perhaps throwing the knee out) and lean your bike into the corner, while keeping the body slightly more upright.
- Around tight bends, brake slightly on approach to (i) give you better traction and (ii) enable you to respond quickly if you need to brake more sharply to negotiate unforeseen hazards that may lie around the bend.
- In cycling through rough areas of sand, gravel, dirt or uneven surface, try to brake in advance. On reaching an area of poor traction, keep a firm grip on the handlebars, place your feet at a position of equal height and do not further engage the brakes.
- Where traffic allows, use apexing to straighten out corners – set up your line from the outside of the road well in advance of the corner, aiming to take the corner at the apex (mid-point) of the road, finally returning to the outside of the road when it straightens up after the bend.

Using this guide

This is a guide to tackling southern Scotland's best road hillclimbs. The aim is to encourage cyclists to embrace road hillclimbing and to provide the information they need to prepare for each climb.

It is not suggested that these are the toughest climbs in southern Scotland,

although the vast majority found here would make it onto such a list. Nor is the compilation limited to the short, sharp climbs that are the mainstay of the road hillclimbs race circuit in southern Scotland. Space prevents the inclusion of Kingscavil, Cult Brae, Stow Hill and other staples of the circuit.

Instead, this guide introduces the cyclist to the diversity of all that southern Scotland has to offer. There are concave climbs that get progressively more difficult toward the summit (Bransly Hill above Dunbar) and convex climbs from which the cyclist spends the latter part recovering from the initial exertion on the steepest pitch (Pease Bay in Berwickshire). Then there are short, sharp bursts up steep escarpments (Gleniffer Braes above Paisley) and long rides over undulating hills (to Mainslaughter Law from Duns).

There are busy urban roads (The Granites, largely on the A7), rural tourist routes (Duke's Pass at Aberfoyle) and quiet country roads (Ross Road on the Isle of Arran); celebrated roads (the Rest and be Thankful) and roads well off the beaten track (High Auldgirth). There are roads rising up from the coast (Braid Fell, near Stranraer) and roads topping out at mountain summits (Lowther Hill above Wanlockhead).

The climbs span the length and breadth of southern Scotland and are organised by region – around Glasgow, the Clyde Coast, Ayrshire and the southwest coast, Dumfries

& Galloway, Border Country, around Edinburgh and the Central Lowlands. Routes include remote outposts such as Wanlockhead and Carter's Bar, as well as the outskirts of the towns and cities of Glasgow, Edinburgh, Stirling, Paisley, Greenock and Ayr.

Each route contains a brief overview of the climb and key data – distance, total ascent, elevation range, average gradient, map grid references for the definitive start and end points, and the relevant OS Landranger map. There's also information on the nearest access by public transport.

The route text identifies key landmarks and hazards that need to be negotiated along the way and highlights the 'killer climb' – the most challenging part of each ascent. A contoured sketch map shows the route and its key features.

At the end of this guide, you'll find a stat page, listing the climbs in rank order by gradient and summarising the length of the climb and total ascent.

The decision on how to approach each climb is left to you. If you are looking at each route as an independent challenge, you'll find everything you need in this volume. If you prefer to tackle some road climbs as part of a longer day out, Pocket Mountains' **Bike Scotland** series makes a useful companion to many of these routes.

Final words

There is a healthy debate among the cycling community on the value and necessity of wearing helmets. If you are undecided, then consider that a helmet won't diminish the thrills of hillclimbing and it may even help you focus less on the danger of descending. Protect that precious cargo with a well-fitted helmet!

Robert Millar, the only Briton to win the King of the Mountains in the Tour de France, grew up in Glasgow and spent his formative cycling years escaping the city to learn his trade. The city itself is a series of little hills known as drumlins (glacial deposits left behind after the last Ice Age), which gives rise to some significant urban challenges, such as the short, sharp 20% climbs up Scott, Montrose and West Campbell Streets in the city centre (best left for a Sunday morning when there are fewer commuters and shoppers in the streets). However, Glasgow's primary attraction for the road hillclimber is that it is an ideal base from which to access some of southern Scotland's toughest road climbs. Glasgow sits in the valley of the River Clyde and the slopes that rise to the north and south of the city present the challenges of the Crow Road and Tak Ma Doon to the north and Gleniffer Braes and Cathkin Braes to the south. Further afield, but still within easy reach of Glasgow, there are other adventures to be had. To the east awaits a series of short but brutal slopes leading to the summit of the Black Hill Transmitter; to the west is the long haul up to the iconic Rest and be Thankful.

6 Lochgoilhead

Balloch

1 Lennoxtown

5 Kilsyth

GLASGOW

Paisley

3

Airdrie 4

2

East Kilbride

AROUND GLASGOW

THE CROW ROAD CAMPSIE FELLS

Distance 3.5 miles/5.7km
Total Height Gain 896ft/273m
Altitude Range 210-1106ft/64-337m
Average Gradient 4.8%
Start A891/B822 junction in Lennoxtown
(NS 626780)
End Road bend (NS 630820)
Map OS Landranger 64
Rail Lenzie Station (5.3 miles),
Milngavie Station (8.8 miles)

**Used in cycling club runs, Time Trials
and hillclimb championships, the Crow
Road from Lennoxtown is a steady climb
across and beyond the Campsie Fells.**

The initial ascent away from the road
junction at the start of Lennoxtown's
Crosshill Street (B822) eases on approach to
a wide, sweeping left-hand bend. Around

the bend, at the end of a small open area,
the Crow Road starts with a 90° turn to the
right. Gentle climbing follows until you
reach the outskirts of Lennoxtown. The now
tree-lined road steepens markedly beyond
Campsie Golf Club on approach to a bend
that turns sharply left, then right. The
incline is less severe after the bend to the
right and it eases further as it approaches a
sweeping left-hand bend. Beyond this is the
long climb up the face of the Campsie
escarpment.

With a kerb on the downside of the slope,
the road is in good condition and wide
enough to warrant central road markings.
Generally straight with excellent forward
vision, there is a kink in the climb halfway
up the escarpment (right, then left), with
the gradient picking up marginally on
approach to the first kink and dropping
slightly on approach to the second. From
here, the downslope is bordered by an
intermittent crash barrier.

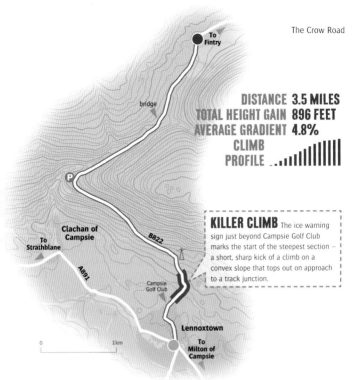

DISTANCE 3.5 MILES
TOTAL HEIGHT GAIN 896 FEET
AVERAGE GRADIENT 4.8%
CLIMB PROFILE

KILLER CLIMB The ice warning sign just beyond Campsie Golf Club marks the start of the steepest section – a short, sharp kick of a climb on a convex slope that tops out on approach to a track junction.

The incline becomes more marked as the road sweeps to the right on approach to the Crow Road car park and viewpoint. The crash barrier returns on the left after this point and the road, now slightly narrower and rougher in quality, ascends the hillside above the river that flows down the valley floor. A flat step is encountered soon after turning the corner, before passing a short crash barrier to the right, with the incline stiffening beyond. This gradient continues until the end of the crash barrier to the left. Unexpectedly, road quality improves beyond here.

Further on, the road narrows after crossing a bridge, and a landscape of rough grassland opens up on either side. The road continues to rise, although much less markedly than before the bridge, first through two tight bends and then through four wide, sweeping bends. The summit is reached before two ice warning signs directed at traffic approaching from the Carron Valley.

13

GLENIFFER BRAES PAISLEY

Distance 1.75 miles/2.8km
Total Height Gain 584ft/178m
Altitude Range 138-722ft/42-220m
Average Gradient 6.3%
Start Road junction by petrol station in Paisley (NS 470617)
End Under pylons (NS 457597)
Map OS Landranger 64
Rail Paisley Gilmour Street Station (2.5 miles)

This climb to the highest point of the Braes above Paisley involves a technically challenging switchback away from the more popular route to the Robertson car park, and an ever-changing gradient on its upper slope.

Leave behind the petrol station on Paisley's Gleniffer Road (B775) for a stiff climb on this straight road. The gradient lessens on reaching the traffic island at the

high flats and eases further at the crossroads beyond. Soon after, you leave the built-up area behind as the road steepens around a left-hand bend to enter Gleniffer Braes Country Park.

For much of this section, the climb is challenging and vision is obscured to the right by a wall/high fence, and to the left by hedges and trees. Only intermittent views across the Clyde Estuary below right can be glimpsed through breaks in the border. The road sweeps to the right, steepening further on the bend. From here, there are several abrupt changes in gradient as the road winds its way to the foot of a longer straight. At a kink to the left halfway up the straight, there is a return to stiff climbing up to the road junction.

Turn sharp left. This switchback turn should, if possible, be approached from the midpoint of the B775 to join the minor road

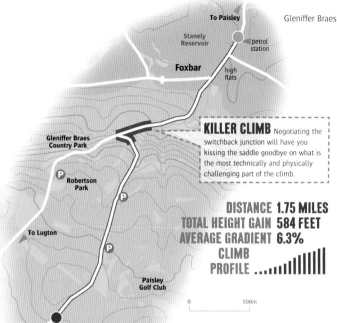

To Paisley

Stanely Reservoir

petrol station

Foxbar

high flats

Gleniffer Braes Country Park

KILLER CLIMB Negotiating the switchback junction will have you kissing the saddle goodbye on what is the most technically and physically challenging part of the climb.

P **Robertson Park**

P

To Lugton

P

Paisley Golf Club

DISTANCE 1.75 MILES
TOTAL HEIGHT GAIN 584 FEET
AVERAGE GRADIENT 6.3%
CLIMB PROFILE ....▁▃▄▅▆▇██

0   500m

at its apex, avoiding the severity of the incline on the inside bend. Poorer road quality exacerbates the challenge.

Although the climb around the switchback eases off a few yards after the turn, the road continues to rise steeply. Initially fringed by plantation forest, two short straights, each followed by a right-hand bend, bring the road to a point where it ascends the hillside more directly. This at first comprises five steps, each levelling off with a momentary flat before resuming the climb. The stepped ascent ends at the second left-hand bend, a

little beyond the point where the forest cover ends, and the gradient eases from here to the roadside car park.

Climbing away, the road bends first to the right, then to the left, topping out at the left-hand bend. The incline stiffens on the straight that ensues, levelling off on reaching the off-road car park. Soon after entering the straight stretch of tree-lined road, there is a return to tougher climbing. Towards the end of the tree cover, following bends to the left and right, the gradient begins to ease off in stages. The summit is gained soon after leaving the tree cover, on passing under a second, smaller line of overhead pylons.

CATHKIN BRAES SOUTH GLASGOW

Distance 3.5 miles/5.6km
Total Height Gain 659ft/201m
Altitude Range 46-646ft/14-197m
Average Gradient 3.6%
Start Clydeford Road, off roundabout at A763/B759 (NS 645613)
End Indistinct summit beyond Cathkin Golf Club (NS 616583)
Map OS Landranger 64
Rail Cambuslang Station (0.5 miles), Carmyle Station (0.75 miles)

Although traffic lights and a difficult crossing over a dual carriageway must be negotiated, the views of Greater Glasgow from the summit make the climb to Cathkin Braes worth the effort.

From the roundabout south of the River Clyde, between Carmyle and Cambuslang, the twin-laned Clydeford Road sweeps gently to the left and steepens gradually on approach to Cambuslang's disused fire station. After a short flat, climb gently to the traffic lights at the road end. Turn right to join Cambuslang Main Street (A724). The gradient picks up on approach to another set of traffic lights.

Turn left to join Greenlees Road (B759 to East Kilbride). On passing the police station to the left, the road dips down momentarily, approaching Cambuslang Institute. From here, the incline picks up, then steepens markedly on bending to the right and passing a sign warning of a 10% gradient. This steep road turns 90° to the right beyond Kirkhill Railway Station, and the gradient slackens. After a second 90° turn, this time to the left, it returns to a 10% climb, topping out at Kirkburn Avenue. Beyond this point, the climb is gentler and the cycling pleasant as the road sweeps around several bends in a verdant residential neighbourhood to reach the

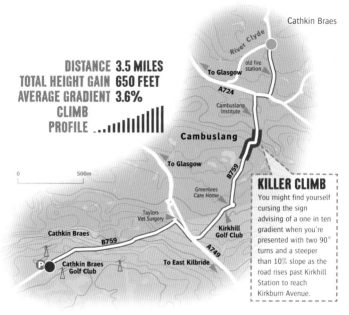

DISTANCE 3.5 MILES
TOTAL HEIGHT GAIN 650 FEET
AVERAGE GRADIENT 3.6%
CLIMB
PROFILE

KILLER CLIMB

You might find yourself cursing the sign advising of a one in ten gradient when you're presented with two 90° turns and a steeper than 10% slope as the road rises past Kirkhill Station to reach Kirkburn Avenue.

roundabout at Greenlees Care Home.

Take the third turning, signposted Greenlees Road, to continue on the B759, heading in the direction of East Kilbride. From here, the road narrows slightly and the surface – while good – is not as smooth as before. Beyond Kirkhill Golf Club, Glasgow can be glimpsed above the low hedgerows. Approaching the end of this road, move to the outside lane to prepare for crossing the dual carriageway (A749). The road bends sharply to the right, then left on approach.

Patience may be required as this is a busy road. While waiting, take in the panoramic views down toward Glasgow, across to the Campsie Fells and back across North

Lanarkshire. After the crossing, the road heads downhill to reach the turn-off to the left where you rejoin the B759 for Carmunnock.

From here, the gradient changes several times, with three distinct ascents: between this junction and Rannoch Wynd; on approach to the road to South Cathkin Farm; and after the sharp bend to the left soon after this junction. Walls, housing and trees obscure views throughout, although these are occasionally breached to give glimpses of Glasgow down below. After Cathkin Braes Golf Club, the summit of the climb is reached at an indistinct point a short distance beyond the double-parking place on the right.

BLACK HILL TRANSMITTER PLAINS

Distance 2.5 miles/4.05km
Total Height Gain 499ft/152m
Altitude Range 509-886ft/155-270m
Average Gradient 3.8%
Start Bridge over Calder Water (NS 798666)
End Road/track junction (NS 827647)
Maps OS Landranger 64 and 65
Rail Drumgelloch Station (1.6 miles)

This route to the Black Hill Transmitter is an unusual climb of almost 500ft, with five ascents and four descents.

Leaving the bridge over the Calder Water at the foot of the new road towards Easter Moffat Golf Club, this tree-fringed road swings sharply to the right for a severe climb past the golf club entrance. The gradient eases as the road leaves the shelter of the trees and negotiates a chicane (right, left, right) before straightening on approach to Easter Moffat Farm.

Beyond the farm, a short dip brings the road down to a 90° bend to the left, a brief straight, flat section leading to a second 90° bend, this time to the right. From this bend, the road steepens markedly as it cuts through Easter Moffat golf course to the road junction at the top.

Turn left to enjoy an all too brief stretch of flat, recently resurfaced road, before turning off to the right to join the rougher road to the Black Hill Transmitter. This mid section of the climb involves more descent than ascent. Views open up ahead over the Moffat Hills towards the Black Hill Transmitter. A long descent takes the road, now only sparsely lined with trees, to the foot of Lochhill, sweeping down through several wide bends.

On crossing a bridge, curve to the right to begin an abrupt climb towards Lochill Farm, reached after a sharp left-hand bend and

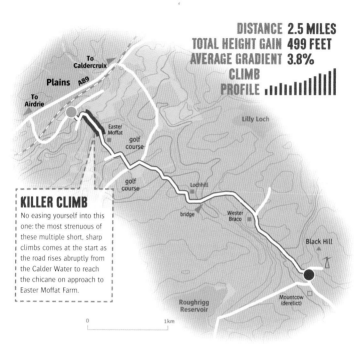

DISTANCE 2.5 MILES
TOTAL HEIGHT GAIN 499 FEET
AVERAGE GRADIENT 3.8%
CLIMB PROFILE

KILLER CLIMB

No easing yourself into this one: the most strenuous of these multiple short, sharp climbs comes at the start as the road rises abruptly from the Calder Water to reach the chicane on approach to Easter Moffat Farm.

then a short flat at the top. From here, descend to a left-hand bend and then more gently down to a hidden bridge over a moorland burn.

The climb away from the bridge starts with a convex slope of three gradients, bringing the road to a sharper right-hand bend, from which follows a gentle descent toward Wester Bracco Farm. A gear change is required to negotiate the steep haul up to

the farm. The road continues to rise past the farm and tops out at a gate, before one last descent on a concave slope brings the road to the foot of the final ascent. This comprises three short, steep climbs, interspersed with flats and less significant rises. The summit is reached at the gate on the left-hand side of the Z-bend (left, right) just before the start of the track branching off to the transmitter.

TAK MA DOON KILSYTH HILLS

Distance 2.6 miles/4.2km
Total Height Gain 869ft/265m
Altitude Range 194-1056ft/59-322m
Average Gradient 6.4%
Start A803/unclassified road junction, Kilsyth (NS 720782)
End Beyond viewpoint car park at summit (NS 734812)
Map OS Landranger 64
Rail Croy Station (2.5 miles)

Following the route of the old drovers' road to Stirling, Tak Ma Doon seems to endlessly wind its way up and across the Campsie Fells escarpment, giving a very different climbing experience to that of the Crow Road at Lennoxtown.

Tak Ma Doon is signposted from the A803 in Kilsyth and starts with a gentle swing to the left and a gradual incline on a well-surfaced twin-track road. The gradient steepens on approach to a sharp right-hand bend, after which the road narrows. This opening climb becomes less hard-going after passing the distinctive white Garrell Mill House. The road continues to rise, with further gradient changes at the National Speed Limit Sign and just before the start of the hedgerow opposite, eventually topping out before the entrance to Beltmoss Quarry.

Here, the road dips briefly, before rising past the picturesque North Lodge of the Colzium Estate. Keeping to the estate boundary, this ascent is gradual and stepped, becoming less marked after a sweeping left-hand bend. Bordering the golf course, the road levels before the entrance to Riskend Quarry. Views of the Campsie Fells can be enjoyed as the incline from here is gentle on a straight stretch of road.

Further on, the road sweeps to the right. Road quality is poorer from here, although some roadside gaps have been rock-filled. The climb away from the bend is taxing and remains so until Brockieside cottage. Forward vision is also limited, on account of

P viewpoint car park

KILLER CLIMB

The opening and closing climbs are stiff, although the short, sharp shock of a climb after Berryhill Farm will have you clicking down through the gears at a faster rate.

Berryhill

Brocketside

golf course

Riskend Quarry

Belmont Quarry

North Lodge Gatehouse

Colzium Estate

Garrell Mill House

To Kirkintilloch

A803

To Falkirk

Kilsyth

0   500m

DISTANCE 2.6 MILES
TOTAL HEIGHT GAIN 869 FEET
AVERAGE GRADIENT 6.4%
CLIMB PROFILE ....|||||

roadside banking and high stone walls on either side. From Brockieside to Berryhill Farm, this improves and the aspect opens up as the road continues to wind its way up the hill.

At the brow of the hill, to the left beyond Berryhill, the road dips down to the foot of a right-hand bend. A sharp ascent follows, comprising a brief straight and a shorter, steeper section of road that lies around a 90° bend to the left. The road drops down to

cross a bridge for some immediate respite, but there is a return to stiff climbing leading up to a right-hand bend that changes the direction of travel for the final ascent.

The gradient eases to a steady climb across the hillside, with the road initially hemmed in by forest cover and a steep embankment. As the road sweeps to the left, the profile of the climb changes once more. The final ascent to the summit comprises three short, steep climbs, interspersed with flats and less significant rises. The summit is reached at the brow of the hill, just beyond the tree-lined viewpoint car park. Take time to enjoy the vista from the viewpoint which, on a clear day, stretches as far as the Forth Bridges.

REST AND BE THANKFUL LOCHGOILHEAD

Distance 2.7 miles/4.33km
Total Height Gain 866ft/264m
Altitude Range 112-978ft/34-298m
Average Gradient 6.1%
Start B839/B828 junction north of Lochgoilhead (NN 192049)
End Road bend (NN 226067)
Map OS Landranger 56
Rail Tarbet Station (13.9 miles), Dalmally Station (37 miles)

The ascent of the Rest and be Thankful from Lochgoilhead is not entirely devoid of traffic, but it presents a less stressful climb with far fewer HGVs and PGVs than the climbs either side of the pass along the busy A83.

The Rest and be Thankful is one of Scotland's iconic road hillclimbs and will be familiar to many readers of this guide. In addition to the ascents from Arrochar and Cairndow, there is also enough left of the old military road up Glen Croe for a testing road hillclimb challenge. Each has its particular merit, but it is the quieter and steeper ascent from Lochgoilhead on the B828, a single-track road of good quality, that is described here.

Leaving the B839/B828 road junction north of Lochgoilhead, the climb is gentle in the lower reaches. Here, the road is tightly hemmed in by forest plantation to the right and deciduous woodland to the left. An initial bend to the right is followed by a long straight, along which the road climbs in steps over a series of knolls, some with intervening dips. There are striking views above and ahead to Beinn an

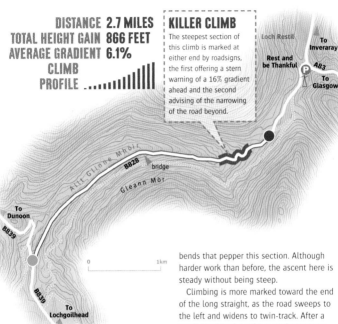

DISTANCE 2.7 MILES
TOTAL HEIGHT GAIN 866 FEET
AVERAGE GRADIENT 6.1%
CLIMB
PROFILE

KILLER CLIMB

The steepest section of this climb is marked at either end by roadsigns, the first offering a stern warning of a 16% gradient ahead and the second advising of the narrowing of the road beyond.

Lochain, although the undulations afford little clear forward vision and extra care is required if traffic is heavy.

Crossing a bridge over the Allt Glinne Mhoir, the climb changes direction and the landscape begins to open up as the woodland border recedes from the roadside now fringed with rough grassland. There are views of the road higher up the hillside, although forward vision does not stretch too far ahead of the front wheel on the small

bends that pepper this section. Although harder work than before, the ascent here is steady without being steep.

Climbing is more marked toward the end of the long straight, as the road sweeps to the left and widens to twin-track. After a small bend to the right, a roadsign warns that the climb ahead is 16%. Soon after the sign, there are a couple of tight bends and the road steepens further. Two wider sweeping bends follow, after which the road narrows and the gradient eases.

The road dips briefly at the top, but soon resumes its ascent, albeit of a less severe gradient than before and with some undulations. The true summit is reached after the road sweeps to the left, heading in a northeast direction, before dropping down to the forest track junction.

23

The roads on the raised beaches that hug the coastlines of the islands and mainland of the Firth of Clyde are well known to cyclists. If coastal storms and heavy vehicular traffic can be avoided, the road from Ardrossan in the south to Gourock in the north offers a pleasant day's cycling, while a circumnavigation of Great Cumbrae by bicycle has been enjoyed by families for many years. Less well known are the road hillclimb challenges that rise up from these raised beaches to the hills above, offering unparalleled views of the Firth of Clyde. Dalry Moor is a much more rewarding and challenging climb than its nearby and better-known neighbour, the Haylie Brae, at Largs. The Isle of Arran is well known to cyclists and this chapter features 'The String', the most celebrated of the island's long hillclimbs, and the Ross Road which, despite being the longest climb on the island, is the road less travelled. The attractions of Clyde Coast road hillclimbing are also of the short, sharp shock variety, and the multiple switchbacks of the Serpentine on the Isle of Bute are a particularly good example. Commanding views of the Clyde sea lochs and the northern reaches of the Firth of Clyde from its summit, mean that Lyle Hill in Gourock is thoroughly deserving of its inclusion in this selection.

CLYDE COAST

LYLE HILL GOUROCK

Distance 0.9 miles/1.5km
Total Height Gain 358ft/109m
Altitude Range 26-381ft/8-116m
Average Gradient 7.3%
Start Rail bridge on Lyle Road (NS 255775)
End Between viewpoint on headland and
slope to summit of Lyle Hill (NS 256770)
Map OS Landranger 63
Rail Fort Matilda Station at start

With its trio of switchbacks, the northern
approach to Lyle Hill is the most
technical of the three routes to the
summit, rising swiftly above Gourock to
present commanding views of the sea
lochs and headlands in the upper reaches
of the Firth of Clyde.

Departing from under the railway bridge
on Gourock's Lyle Road, the road climbs

stiffly from the outset on a short straight,
before bending sharply to the right.
Now passing through a residential
neighbourhood, the width of the twin-track
road enables street-parked cars to be
negotiated without difficulty. A minor twist
(left, then right) is soon followed by a
marked switchback to the left. The incline
steepens around the switchback and
remains steep on the straight that separates
it from a second hairpin bend to the right.
Once more, the road steepens around this,
although less markedly than before as the
direction of travel is now on the outer bend.
As the road straightens, there is a subtle
reduction in the gradient.

No sooner has the road straightened than
it starts a broad sweep to the left, which
brings it to the foot of a long straight.

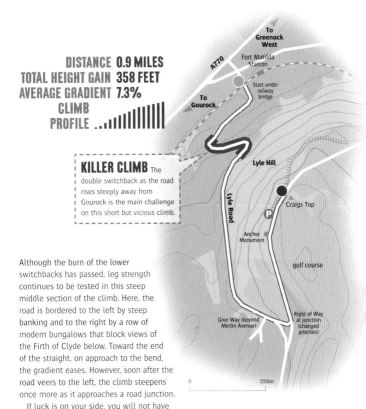

DISTANCE 0.9 MILES
TOTAL HEIGHT GAIN 358 FEET
AVERAGE GRADIENT 7.3%
CLIMB PROFILE

KILLER CLIMB The double switchback as the road rises steeply away from Gourock is the main challenge on this short but vicious climb.

Although the burn of the lower switchbacks has passed, leg strength continues to be tested in this steep middle section of the climb. Here, the road is bordered to the left by steep banking and to the right by a row of modern bungalows that block views of the Firth of Clyde below. Toward the end of the straight, on approach to the bend, the gradient eases. However, soon after the road veers to the left, the climb steepens once more as it approaches a road junction.

If luck is on your side, you will not have to give way to traffic at the Merlin Avenue junction and you can continue the stiff climb without adding the burden of a standing start. Keeping to the left after the junction, you have right of way to negotiate the final switchback and, with a steep shift to the left, change the direction of climb.

From here, the ascent is steady but less intense. The open aspect to the left affords pleasing views of Gourock Bay. Beyond the monumental anchor, the road sweeps gently to the right and tops out on the road between the lower headland to the left and the summit of Lyle Hill to the right.

27

THE SERPENTINE ROTHESAY, BUTE

Distance 0.85 miles/1.3km
Total Height Gain 367ft/112m
Altitude Range 7-374ft/2-114m
Average Gradient 8.3%
Start West Princes Street/Bishop Street junction in Rothesay (NS 090647)
End Beyond road/track junction (NS 098644)
Map OS Landranger 63
Rail Ferry to Rothesay from Wemyss Bay; connecting trains from Glasgow Central

A quirky climb of multiple switchbacks that is the signature race in Bute's annual Festival of Cycling weekend. Outstanding views of Rothesay Bay are ample reward for what might just be the slowest three-quarters of a mile you have ever cycled.

From the town centre, leave the junction with West Princes Street to climb gently to the end of Bishop Street. The incline increases gently from the midpoint of this straight. Turn sharp left on reaching Castle Street to confront the first of 11 switchbacks that snake up the wall of hillside known locally as the Serpentine. You are surrounded on either side by grand villas that hark back to Rothesay's heyday as the playground of rich merchants from the industrial towns of west Scotland.

Four short switchbacks are traversed in the lower part of the climb, which ends as the route cuts across Mount Pleasant Road to continue with another seven switchbacks to reach the halfway point!

The gaps between switchbacks lengthen

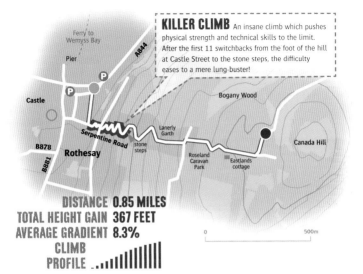

KILLER CLIMB An insane climb which pushes physical strength and technical skills to the limit. After the first 11 switchbacks from the foot of the hill at Castle Street to the stone steps, the difficulty eases to a mere lung-buster!

DISTANCE 0.85 MILES
TOTAL HEIGHT GAIN 367 FEET
AVERAGE GRADIENT 8.3%
CLIMB
PROFILE

as the climb progresses, but are not long enough to offer much compensation for tiring legs faced with ever-steepening hairpin bends. This section of ascent ends as the grassy hillside is left behind on completing a left switchback, across the road from a now redundant set of stone steps.

In the section that follows, the climbing is just as demanding, although the longer straights mean that it is now less technically challenging. There is also a change in aspect as the road is hemmed in by the high stone boundary walls of the villas on these upper slopes.

At the end of the first straight, there is a staged switchback of two right bends separated by a short straight that rises directly up the hill. Beyond, another longer

straight is followed by two switchbacks (left, then right), before a sharp bend to the left reaches the foot of a steep straight that climbs up past a caravan park to a T-junction.

Turn left here, followed by a sharp right to continue climbing, now more gently. Once you are past Roseland Lodge Caravan Park, the good-quality road rises through farmland on either side. At the end of the straight, the road steepens on approach to a sharp right-hand bend, which is shortly followed by a switchback to the left and then a chicane (left, right, left). The gradient eases on reaching a cottage. Now rising very gently, the road bends sharply to the left at the gate that takes walkers to the summit of Canada Hill. The road tops out at an indistinct point a few yards beyond.

THE STRING BRODICK, ARRAN

Distance 1.9 miles/3.3km
Total Height Gain 741ft/226m
Altitude Range 26-768ft/8-234m
Average Gradient 7.3%
Start B880/A841 junction north of Brodick (NS 005368)
End First snow pole beyond solar mast (NR 978358)
Map OS Landranger 69
Rail Ferry to Brodick from Ardrossan; connecting trains from Glasgow Central

The most notable climb on an island revered for its road cycling starts briskly and ends steeply, with a long steady ascent in between.

The B880 String Road, or 'The String' as it is also known, cuts over Arran's mountainous interior from Brodick to Blackwaterfoot. Climb sharply away from the A841/B880 junction north of Brodick on the initially poor-quality twin-track B880. Beyond the turn-off towards Glen Rosa on the right, the road sweeps left, then right as it skirts the edge of the cemetery and follows the line of the forest. Beyond the cemetery, it bends sharply to the left and, soon after this, the gradient eases and road quality improves.

The long straight section of road that follows gives outstanding views towards Glen Rosa and the majestic peak of Goatfell to the right, although only glimpses are initially possible over the large hedge and through intermittent breaks in tree cover. Brief respite from the steady climb is offered by a series of dips, but these also crank up the difficulty as the

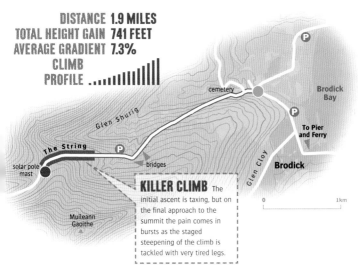

DISTANCE 1.9 MILES
TOTAL HEIGHT GAIN 741 FEET
AVERAGE GRADIENT 7.3%
CLIMB PROFILE

KILLER CLIMB The initial ascent is taxing, but on the final approach to the summit the pain comes in bursts as the staged steepening of the climb is tackled with very tired legs.

gradient stiffens away from the foot of each.

A double bend breaks up the straight further on. Beyond these bends, the road straightens out and the trees on the right disappear, affording a clear view toward the head of Glen Shurig. On passing the second of two small stone bridges, there is a marked change of direction and the road dips to cross a larger bridge with parking places and a viewpoint. It is worth pausing to take in the views down Glen Shurig towards Brodick Castle and across the hills to Goatfell.

The final ascent up The String begins sharply on a straight of very good quality, with open aspect on both sides. Along this

stretch of road, views gradually open up to the right towards the famous A'Chir Ridge. This section comprises three short climbs and two steps, these steps representing reductions in gradient rather than downward dips, with more significant climbing being evident after the first step. The white snowpoles mark the start of the second climb and this is clearly the most taxing of the three. The brief respite at the second step is followed by a final, challenging climb. Beyond the road bend to the left, the gradient eases after the solar-powered mast. The summit is reached on passing the snowpole on the opposite side of the road.

THE ROSS ROAD LAMLASH, ARRAN

Distance 2.1 miles/3.4km
Total Height Gain 869ft/265m
Altitude Range 66-935ft/20-285m
Average Gradient 7.8%
Start Road/track junction west of Lamlash
(NS 017301)
End Cattle grid (NR 987294)
Map Landranger 69
Rail Ferry to Brodick from Ardrossan;
connecting trains from Glasgow Central

**The highest road hillclimb on the Isle of
Arran comprises a long steady rise on a
single-track road which reaches the
summit after a viciously steep ascent on
its lower slope.**

Climb gently away from the junction with
the track leading to Glenkiln Farm on the
unclassified Ross Road, which heads for the
hills having left the A841 on the outskirts of
Lamlash. The incline picks up briefly after
the blue Sustrans sign for a cycle forest
track to Kilmory. An equally short but much
gentler section of ascent takes the road up
to a cattle grid

Now the climbing starts in earnest.
The road is soon hemmed in by plantation
forest to the left and a high bank of
deciduous woodland to the right. Ten bends
are negotiated as the road weaves steeply
up the hillside above the Monamore Glen.
There is little forward vision, and the
occasional crash barrier to the left is a
reminder of the need for due care. This part
of the climb concludes where the roadside
banking and the plantation forest end. Here,
a new forest track enters a large swathe of
recently felled forest that stretches to the
far side of the northernmost bend of the
Ross Road climb. Views now open up as the

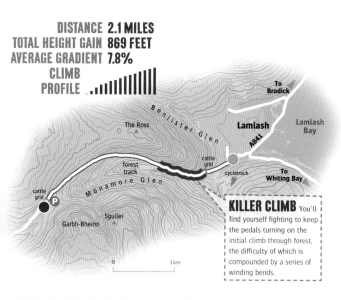

DISTANCE 2.1 MILES
TOTAL HEIGHT GAIN 869 FEET
AVERAGE GRADIENT 7.8%
CLIMB PROFILE

To Brodick

Benlister Glen

The Ross

Lamlash

Lamlash Bay

A841

cattle grid

cycletrack

To Whiting Bay

forest track

Monamore Glen

cattle grid

P

Sguiler

Garbh-Bheinn

0   1km

KILLER CLIMB You'll find yourself fighting to keep the pedals turning on the initial climb through forest, the difficulty of which is compounded by a series of winding bends.

route rises steadily above the felled forest on a straight road with the few kinks failing to impair forward vision.

There are ample passing places and a few parking spots. The route follows the shape of the hillside, gradually changing direction to travel southwest. The line of the hillside above the road to the right can be traced to approximate the summit, which lies beyond the plantation forest that reappears further on. On approach to the edge of this plantation, there is a subtle increase in the gradient – this steeper section of road climbing persisting until a little way

after the start of a forest clearing.

From here, the route to the summit is a much gentler climb on a road of variable quality. The plantation forest is set further back, affording open aspect on both sides, and the road is generally straight with good forward vision. The summit is reached at a cattle grid soon after the large parking and picnic area and just before the start of another band of plantation forest on the opposite side of the road. The reward from the summit is a spectacular view back toward Lamlash Bay and the Holy Isle – best enjoyed from the picnic area.

DALRY MOOR AYRSHIRE

Distance 2 miles/3.3km
Total Height Gain 791ft/241m
Altitude Range 33-810ft/10-247m
Average Gradient 7.3%
Start A78/unclassified road junction south of Fairlie (NS 205530)
End Before cattle grid (NS 227523)
Map OS Landranger 63
Rail Fairlie Station (1.1 miles)

A Scottish Hillclimb Championship road that rises in two miles to give spectacular views of the Firth of Clyde and the Clyde Islands. The industrial landscape of Hunterston, largely and effectively hidden from view at sea level, is laid bare for all to see.

Leave the busy A78 south of Fairlie at Fencebay Fisheries, taking the moor road which starts innocuously enough with a gentle climb, passing under two bridges before meeting a 90° bend to the right. From the bend, the road narrows to single track and, with trees tightly enclosing it on either side, follows a short straight to a second 90° bend, this time to the left.

The road flattens up to the Fairlie Furniture Works. A stiff climb on a road bounded by high hedgerows follows, persisting through the left-hand bend until a fence joins the roadside hedge to the left, midway up a long straight. Despite the reduction in gradient, the climbing remains stiff. Soon bordered by plantation forest, the gradient eases further at a wide, sweeping right-hand bend, the less severe incline continuing past a left-hand bend until it tops out where the plantation forest ends and a narrow band of trees joins the roadside.

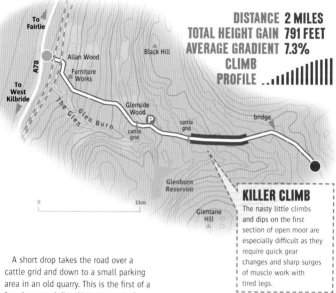

DISTANCE **2 MILES**
TOTAL HEIGHT GAIN **791 FEET**
AVERAGE GRADIENT **7.3%**
CLIMB
PROFILE

KILLER CLIMB

The nasty little climbs and dips on the first section of open moor are especially difficult as they require quick gear changes and sharp surges of muscle work with tired legs.

A short drop takes the road over a cattle grid and down to a small parking area in an old quarry. This is the first of a few downward dips. Now narrower, the borderless road has frequent passing places and offers good forward vision as it cuts through open moorland.

Veering to the right, the road climbs sharply away from the old quarry. This tough climb on a generally straight stretch of road ends as the road dips down over a second cattle grid to cross a burn. From here to the lower top, the climb profile is complex. Two short, stiff pitches, interspersed by a flat, precede a steadier incline. Then a left-hand bend marks the start of two dips, between

which lies a short, sharp climb. This is also followed by a steady ascent, bringing the road to the lower top.

From here, the road drops down to sweep widely on a right-hand bend and cross the Whiteside Burn at the Knockendon Bridge. A long steady climb ensues, then a gentler gradient and a brief dip. Away from the dip, a convex slope takes the road to its highest point at a left-hand bend, before it starts to descend towards the cattle grid a short distance beyond.

Irvine

1

Ayr

2

Maybole

3

Girvan

Barr

4

5

Stranraer

For many years, the coastal towns of South Ayrshire offered respite for merchants and workers from Glasgow and the large industrial towns of central Scotland. More recently, generations of road cyclists have come to associate southwest Scotland with The Girvan, Scotland's premier tour event which was held every spring until 2009. Many of the area's best climbs start by the sea, taking the cyclist up into the hills above, which in turn provide commanding views of the coastline below. The two best examples of coast to hillclimbs are Dundonald Hill and Brown Carrick Hill, both of which are isolated local landmarks, well known to local cyclists and, in the case of Brown Carrick Hill, to those following National Cycle Route 7 from Carlisle to Glasgow (Lochs & Glens South). Nick o' the Balloch and the Black Hill of Garleffin will be known to those who are familiar with The Girvan, although their inclusion in this selection was by no means a given, considering the array of road hillclimbing available in the area. The extremities of the region also have something to offer the road hillclimber, and Braid Fell is a worthy addition to the set.

AYRSHIRE AND THE SOUTHWEST COAST

DUNDONALD HILL LOANS, TROON

Distance Option A: 1 mile/1.6km
B: 1.85 miles/3km
Total Height Gain A: 348ft/106m
B: 525ft/160m
Altitude Range A: 66-417ft/22-129m
B: 66-492ft/20-150m
Average Gradient A: 6.6% B: 5.4%
Start Mini roundabout for A759, B746 and
Old Loans Road (NS 346316)
End A: beyond parking place (NS 356328)
B: summit transmitter (NS 360325)
Map OS Landranger 70
Rail Troon Station (1.5 miles)

**There are two options for this route:
ascend the measured mile used by local
cyclists in training, or extend this to the
summit of Dundonald Hill. Either way, the
reward is outstanding views of Ayr Bay.**

Both options climb away from the mini
roundabout between Loans and Troon in the
direction of Dundonald/ Highgrove Hotel on
a wide twin-track road of good quality with

central road markings. The gradient
steepens as it approaches the bridge over
the A78 dual carriageway. The road sweeps
to the left and steepens further on
approach to the Highgrove. High hedgerows
on either side obscure views of the
surrounding countryside, but do not impair
forward vision on this straight section of
road. Beyond the hotel, the road swings to
the left, then more sharply to the right as
the midpoint of the climb is reached.

From here, the road is a series of short
straights divided by wide sweeping bends,
with the incline reducing in stages towards
the summit. Views open up across farmland
towards the Isle of Arran and North Ayrshire
– with the best to be gained from the
parking places, particularly the first, on the
left-hand side. The summit of Option A is
finally reached just beyond the second
parking place.

Option B carries on over the summit,
dropping gently at the outset. The descent

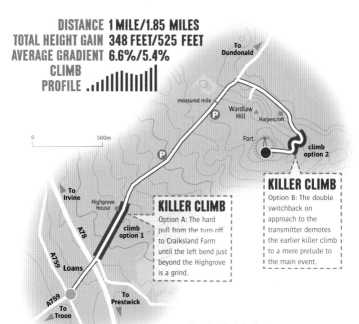

DISTANCE 1 MILE/1.85 MILES
TOTAL HEIGHT GAIN 348 FEET/525 FEET
AVERAGE GRADIENT 6.6%/5.4%
CLIMB PROFILE

measured mile

Wardlaw Hill

Harpercroft

Fort

climb option 2

KILLER CLIMB

Option B: The double switchback on approach to the transmitter demotes the earlier killer climb to a mere prelude to the main event.

KILLER CLIMB

Option A: The hard pull from the turn-off to Craiksland Farm until the left bend just beyond the Highgrove is a grind.

To Dundonald

To Irvine

Highgrove House

A78

A759

Loans

A759

To Troon

To Prestwick

climb option 1

steepens as the road bends right and then left to reach the minor road junction. Turn right, taking care as high hedgerows obscure visibility from traffic at this point. Continue to descend until you pass the gated road that leads to the summit of Wardlaw Hill. Carry on ahead, now on the flat, and take the left fork, following the line of the high hedgerow to bypass Harpercroft Farm. Negotiate a gate that stretches across the road and climb to the far side of Harpercroft Farm, before dropping down briefly to reach a second gate and cattle grid.

Now the climb begins in earnest. The road is very good quality for a summit climb, although you may find your tyres sloshing through cattle manure on some sections. Climb stiffly and directly up the hill to reach a left-hand bend, where the road now rises less severely across the hillside. At the end of this straight, two wide switchbacks (right, then left) take the road to a second cattle grid at a gap in the wall. This is the killer climb of Option B. A short flat is followed by a gentle incline and a final haul up to the gates of the radio transmitter at the summit of Dundonald Hill.

BROWN CARRICK HILL SOUTH OF AYR

Distance 1.6 miles/2.6km
Total Height Gain 745ft/227m
Altitude Range 167-876ft/51-267m
Average Gradient 7.7%
Start A719 road junction (NS 288178)
End Road end at summit (NS 292162)
Map OS Landranger 70
Rail Ayr Station (4.6 miles)

This detour to the summit of Brown Carrick Hill – above what is already a tough climb across the Carrick Hills on National Cycle Route 7 – delivers outstanding views of Ayr.

Leave the A719 coast road south of Ayr to head inland on National Cycle Route 7 with open farmland on either side. The road weaves between the old schoolhouse and Genoch Farm. Beyond, with high hedgerows on either side limiting forward vision, it sweeps to the left, then right before dropping briefly at the start of a long straight leading to a 90° bend to the right. A shorter straight follows, taking you to another 90° bend, this time to the left, to reach the foot of the climb proper.

The road steepens relentlessly on the straight toward the imposing Carwinshoch house, which is reached after two sharp bends (left, then right). A cattle grid is passed soon after the house on a shorter straight which leads to two switchbacks bends (right, then left).

Beyond these, after a sharp shift to the right, the bends become less pronounced as the road winds through gorse bushes. This part of the climb is taxing, but less severe than Carwinshoch's switchbacks. Road quality improves as the hillside opens on both sides, with excellent views towards the

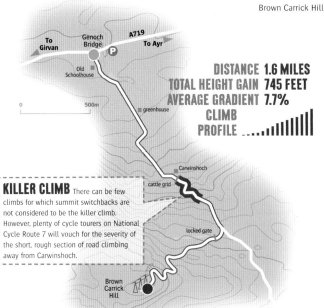

DISTANCE 1.6 MILES
TOTAL HEIGHT GAIN 745 FEET
AVERAGE GRADIENT 7.7%
CLIMB PROFILE

KILLER CLIMB There can be few climbs for which summit switchbacks are not considered to be the killer climb. However, plenty of cycle tourers on National Cycle Route 7 will vouch for the severity of the short, rough section of road climbing away from Carwinshoch.

summit of Brown Carrick Hill. The high point of the climb on National Cycle Route 7 is reached at the knoll beside the feeding troughs (NS 299164), which lies a short distance beyond a more distinctive knoll crowned with a cairn.

The true summit of Brown Carrick rests 225ft above the high point of the hillside road. Soon after reaching the summit plateau, leave the hillside road for the distinctive tree-lined road to the right (NS 297166). A locked gate can be negotiated by either dismounting or following the line of a rough track that leads to a gap in the trees, joining the road further on.

This minor inconvenience aside, the final

climb to the summit is rewarding with alpine-esque qualities. Road quality is excellent and it is highly unlikely that you will encounter any traffic. The climb stiffens as the road peels away from the line of trees and then eases at a bend to the right, which is followed by a long straight. The road swings to the left at the end of this straight and starts to wend its way towards the summit through a series of wide sweeping bends and switchbacks. The final switchback under the rockface is particularly steep. The summit is reached at the gate across the road before the transmitters.

BLACK HILL OF GARLEFFIN
EAST OF GIRVAN

Distance 5.7 miles/9.2km
Total Height Gain 1122ft/342m
Altitude Range 82-1106ft/25-337m
Average Gradient 3.7%
Start Bridge over Water of Girvan between Dailly and Crosshill at Kilkerran (NS 306042)
End Road/track junction (NX 331996)
Map OS Landranger 76
Rail Maybole Station (5 miles), Girvan Station (9.5 miles)

Rising from the Vale of Girvan, Garleffin is a relentless climb at a steady gradient on a single-track road. The difficulty is heightened by the poor-quality road surface and limited forward vision in the lower part. Garleffin forms part of National Cycle Route 7.

Start at the foot of the narrow stone bridge over the Water of Girvan, off the B741 at Kilkerran. An initial climb is followed by an undulating straight which brings the road to a second stone bridge, just past the crossroads at the Walled Garden caravan park. The narrow single-track road then swings to the left with a more marked ascent. At the top, following a bend to the right, there is a return to a long, undulating straight, then a steady climb to reach the T-junction.

Turning right at the junction, the ascent of Garleffin now begins in earnest. The gradient steepens temporarily on the approach to Auchalton Farm. Beyond, a steady climb takes the road up through farmland to reach a junction with the option of diverting to Straiton.

Continue ahead to enjoy an improved section of road, which starts with a gentle climb away from the junction and ends with a more pronounced climb to the row of modern houses set back from the road at Cullochknowes; these climbs are separated by a short flat.

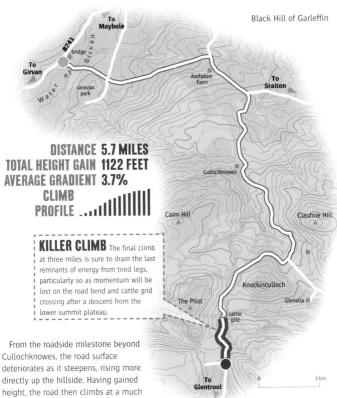

DISTANCE 5.7 MILES
TOTAL HEIGHT GAIN 1122 FEET
AVERAGE GRADIENT 3.7%
CLIMB PROFILE

KILLER CLIMB The final climb at three miles is sure to drain the last remnants of energy from tired legs, particularly so as momentum will be lost on the road bend and cattle grid crossing after a descent from the lower summit plateau.

From the roadside milestone beyond Cullochknowes, the road surface deteriorates as it steepens, rising more directly up the hillside. Having gained height, the road then climbs at a much gentler gradient through an area of recently felled plantation forest, sweeping up through wide bends to reach the junction with the road that branches left toward Glenalla Farm.

Bending to the right after the short straight beyond the Glenalla turn-off, the road climbs and bends to the left to enter a wide firebreak with plantation forest set far back on both sides. The gradient now

lessens to a steady climb towards a lower summit plateau. The road drops downhill to a cattle grid, before making the steep ascent towards the upper summit. This is gained unexpectedly on the straight beyond a left-hand bend – just after a large passing place/parking area on the right at the Doughty Hill junction.

43

NICK O' THE BALLOCH STINCHAR VALLEY

Distance 2.3 miles/3.7km
Total Height Gain 797ft/243m
Altitude Range 479-1276ft/146-389m
Average Gradient 6.5%
Start Unclassified junction between Barr and Glen Trool (NX 330955)
End Second passing place beyond crash barriers at summit (NX 346927)
Map OS Landranger 76
Rail Girvan Station (12.1 miles)

Crash barriers on the down slope near the summit lend dramatic effect to an iconic climb which will be familiar to those who have followed The Girvan. The surface is excellent for a country road and although there are limited passing places, the inconvenience of having to pause to accommodate cars is compensated by stunning views of the surrounding hillside.

Head away from the junction with the valley road to Barr, just south of the River Stinchar, on a straight, good quality, single-track road. The gentle climb through open farmland is part of the Lochs & Glens South cycle route (National Cycle Route 7), this stage connecting Maybole in Ayrshire with Glen Trool in Galloway. Towards Pinvalley Farm at the end of the straight, the gradient steepens. After the farm, the road swings sharply to the left and begins a stiff climb into the forested hillside, away from the valley plain. Passing the entrance to the Galloway Forest Park mountain bike trail, it sweeps left, then sharply to the right as it enters the forest proper.

The road continues to climb as the aspect alternates between mature and nursery forest on either side. Road quality is good and there are frequent passing places. Views open up at two prominent headlands to the

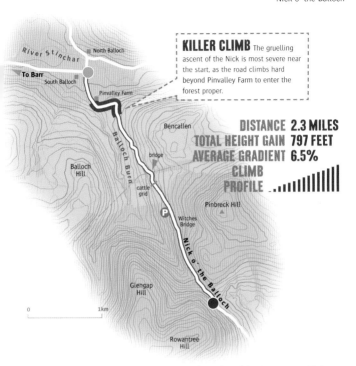

KILLER CLIMB The gruelling ascent of the Nick is most severe near the start, as the road climbs hard beyond Pinvalley Farm to enter the forest proper.

DISTANCE 2.3 MILES
TOTAL HEIGHT GAIN 797 FEET
AVERAGE GRADIENT 6.5%
CLIMB PROFILE

right, both of which precede sharp bends to the left. After the second 'viewpoint', the road passes beneath overhead pylons and reaches a bridge. A sharp climb away from the bridge tops out at a left-hand bend, and the view opens up ahead to crash barriers cutting around the side of the hill at the summit. The road now climbs at a steady rate, crossing a cattle grid as it leaves the forest and approaches a junction.

Soon after, the route crosses Witches Bridge and crash barriers appear, offering a reassuring degree of protection from the steep drop down the hillside and making for a dramatic final stretch of the ascent. The road remains narrow with very few passing places, with the steady gradient persisting as it winds around the side of the hill. The summit is reached at the second passing place to the left beyond the crash barriers, following a gentle climb from the first passing place.

BRAID FELL NORTH OF STRANRAER

Distance 3 miles/4.9km
Total Height Gain 702ft/214m
Altitude Range 49-689ft/15-210m
Average Gradient 4.4%
Start Road/path junction off the A77, north of Stranraer (NX 089639)
End Passing place (NX 106663)
Map OS Landranger 82
Rail Stranraer Station (3 miles)

A fine climb in a part of Scotland not renowned for its hill roads. Although the surrounding countryside on the summit ridge might be described as nondescript and bleak, the views back down toward Stranraer and across Loch Ryan to the headland at Milleur are ample reward for the effort.

Start at the road/path junction a short distance along the unclassified single-track road that branches off from the A77 north of Stranraer. The climb begins gently on a road which maintains its good quality throughout. Bending to the left before a house and further to the left beyond, the road then straightens and steepens towards the end of the straight. Taking a 90° turn to pass between an imposing white country house to the left and Craigcaffie Farm to the right, a short straight is followed by a bend to the left, only to straighten again as the road aims directly for the gorse-clad hillside ahead.

At the foot of the slope, the road turns 90° to the right and rises more steeply across the hillside. Through the hedges on

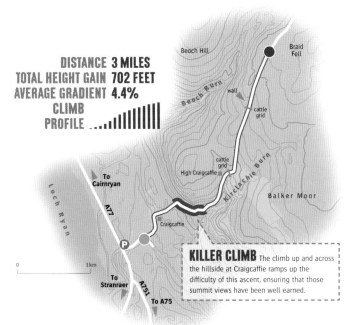

DISTANCE 3 MILES
TOTAL HEIGHT GAIN 702 FEET
AVERAGE GRADIENT 4.4%
CLIMB PROFILE ....ıllıllıll

KILLER CLIMB The climb up and across the hillside at Craigcaffie ramps up the difficulty of this ascent, ensuring that those summit views have been well earned.

the right, the view opens up towards Stranraer. The gradient of the climb eases momentarily at the other side of the hill slope, just beyond the house near the start of plantation forest. The road then changes direction as it sweeps to the left. Tucked in by the hillside with high hedges and plantation forest, the views are closed off at this point and a long section of steady climbing beckons on the approach to High Craigcaffie.

A wide Z-bend (right, then left) follows High Craigcaffie, with a cattle grid to be negotiated on the short straight between the bends. A steady climb on the long straight that follows soon leaves the forest behind. After this straight, as the road veers to the right, the aspect opens up, with a gentler climb towards the summit.

Although the surrounding countryside is bleak, the views back to Loch Ryan are quite spectacular. A second cattle grid is passed on approach to a distinctive 20ft wall, and the summit is reached on the second passing place (the first on the left) beyond the wall.

Dumfries and Galloway brands itself as the 'natural choice for cyclists', inviting them to 'explore the unspoilt landscape'. There is much to suggest that this marketing line is entirely justified. More than 100 miles of the National Cycle Network pass through the county, five of the 7stanes mountain bike Meccas are found within easy reach of Dumfries and the region's Tour DoonHame has taken over from The Girvan, the UK's second longest cycle stage race. Surprisingly, although some of Scotland's longest road climbs are also found here, it is less known for road hillclimbing. Close to Dumfries, High Auldgirth is a gem of a short climb with over 500ft of ascent in little more than one mile. Further to the west, Creetown is better known for its gem rocks than its treasure of a climb from the town to the radio transmitter at the summit of Cambret Hill. The climb to Todholes Hill is also on an approach to a radio transmitter, rising to over 1000ft to offer expansive and seldom-seen views of the Nithsdale Valley below. Best known of all will be the climb that rises away from Sanquhar through the Mennock Pass and up to Glengonnar Halt beyond Wanlockhead. For those with bags of energy, the Mennock Pass and Lowther Hill can be combined for a mega climb of more than 2000ft.

Wanlockhead

Sanquhar

Auldgirth

Dumfries

Creetown

DUMFRIES AND GALLOWAY

1 **Cambret Hill** 50

A long, staged climb of over 1000ft, ending on a road of rough quality leading to the radio transmitter atop Cambret Hill

2 **High Auldgirth** 52

Brace yourself for a short, sharp shock of a climb on a no-through road, comprising three switchbacks and an average gradient of 9.5%

3 **Todholes Hill** 54

A steady ascent toward the radio mast on Todholes Hill, rising to more than 1000ft on a no-through road almost always devoid of traffic

4 **Mennock Pass and Glengonnar Halt** 56

This long climb steepens remorselessly up a narrow river valley to Scotland's highest village of Wanlockhead

5 **Lowther Hill** 58

Over 1000ft of climbing in under three miles to gain the top of Lowther Hill – a unique experience on the best quality hill road that Scotland has to offer

CAMBRET HILL CREETOWN

Distance 4.1 miles/6.5km
Total Height Gain 1161ft/354m
Altitude Range 33-1152ft/10-351m
Average Gradient 5.4%
Start Unclassified road junction in
Creetown (NX 476589)
End Road end at summit (NX 525579)
Map OS Landranger 83
Rail Barrhill Station (25.1 miles), Dumfries
Station (41.7 miles)

**Road quality is poor on the upper part
of this 1000ft climb, and off-road tyres
would be beneficial. The rare sense of
achievement of cycling to a hill summit
awaits those who opt for the final
ascent to the radio transmitter.**

Across from the Ellangowan Hotel on
Creetown's high street, the road to Cambret
Hill is already steep at the outset. Veering
sharply to the left and then more gently to

the right, the road twists its way up through
the town. After Bank Street, take the road to
the right, which is signposted for
Glenquicken Farm Trout Fishery. The gradient
eases on approach to the last of Creetown's
houses. Soon after, the road becomes narrow
single-track, bending sharply to the left to
enter the countryside proper.

Road quality is good and the surface is
even. However, with high hedgerows on
either side, there is a need to remain
vigilant as forward vision is limited with the
road veering to the right around the hillside.
Views begin to open up over the
countryside below as the road passes the
turn-off for the Glenquicken Farm Fishery.

Ahead, the road dips and passes a small
pond, undulating beyond this as it joins and
then skirts the edge of the forest. There is a
more marked descent on approach to the
bridge at the start of forest on the left.

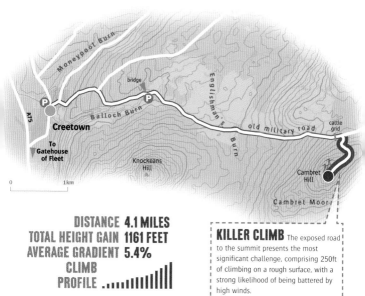

DISTANCE **4.1 MILES**
TOTAL HEIGHT GAIN **1161 FEET**
AVERAGE GRADIENT **5.4%**
CLIMB
PROFILE iiiiilllll

KILLER CLIMB The exposed road to the summit presents the most significant challenge, comprising 250ft of climbing on a rough surface, with a strong likelihood of being battered by high winds.

Climbing steeply beyond the bridge, the road comes to a passing/parking place for the Balloch Community Woodland. Road quality deteriorates as it makes its way around the lochan and then rises more markedly again, with progress hampered by potholes and the rough surface. As the gradient eases, a second series of undulations is encountered before another marked dip as the forest is left behind on approach to a second bridge.

Now with open hillside to the right, Cambret Hill can be viewed clearly. The long, steady climb steepens significantly after bending sharply to cross a third bridge. At the end of this long, steep stretch of road, it emerges onto open moor. The road up to the transmitter is met soon after the cattle grid beyond the forest.

As might be expected, the transmitter road is very rough and the gradient is challenging throughout. It swings to the left after a few hundred yards, followed by a series of wide sweeping bends towards the summit. Once past the main mast, the summit is just beyond the corner of the area enclosed by high barbed wire fencing.

HIGH AULDGIRTH NORTH OF DUMFRIES

Distance 1.2 miles/1.95km
Total Height Gain 607ft/185m
Altitude Range 98-705ft/30-215m
Average Gradient 9.5%
Start Unclassified road junction off the A76, next to the Auldgirth Inn (NX 913865)
End Road end (NX 923878)
Map OS Landranger 78
Rail Dumfries Station (8.4 miles)

A regional championship hillclimb above the Nithsdale Valley, which negotiates three switchbacks and several steep straights from the village of Auldgirth.

The village lies off the A76 about halfway between Dumfries and Thornhill. Climb steeply away from the unclassified road junction on the valley floor, initially on a twin-track road with central markings, but narrowing to single track after the first bend to the left. Beyond, the road climbs steadily but less stiffly, largely on straights but with two further bends (right, then left) to reach a humpback bridge. On the far side, a momentary dip to the foot of a bend to the left precedes a return to climbing, with the gradient steepening as the road bends to the right on approach to the white buildings of Low Auldgirth Farm. The stiff incline continues straight up to the road/track junction.

Turning 90° right, the climb to High Auldgirth begins in earnest. A switchback to the left soon reverses the direction of travel. Road quality is roughest on the steep inside bend of the turn and it would be advisable to climb on the outside if traffic permits. The first of two long

Blackcraig Hill

two humps
across road

High Auldgirth

KILLER CLIMB

The three switchbacks are interspersed
with long straights which climb steeply
up the hillside – together they present
one of the stiffest road hillclimb
challenges in southwest Scotland.

DISTANCE 1.2 MILES
TOTAL HEIGHT GAIN 607 FEET
AVERAGE GRADIENT 9.5%
CLIMB
PROFILE ....ııılIIIIIIII

To
Thornhill

A76

River Nith

Low Auldgirth

0   500m

Auldgirth
To
Dumfries

straights, each of which has a bend to the
right at its midpoint, starts here.

Now enclosed by forest, the road rises
steadily and steeply up the hillside. After a
gentle bend to the right, it leaves the
forest cover behind, opening up views of
the countryside below. At a road/track
junction at the end of the straight, there is
a switchback to the right and the road re-
enters the trees. There is not much time to
recover before the second switchback, this
time to the left.

The second, longer straight begins here.
The forest soon recedes on the left,

affording extensive views across the valley.
Following the course of the hillside, the
road then bends to the right to continue its
steady climb. Further on, at a bend to the
right shortly after re-entering the forest on
the left, the gradient levels out. There's
soon a return to tougher climbing, though,
on approach to a sharp bend to the left,
topping out by a corrugated iron farmshed.

Having levelled off as it passes the shed,
the final ascent starts on approach to a
90° turn to the right at the crossroads. The
final stretch is on a very rough section,
which is straddled by two speed bumps at
either end of the row of timber-framed
bungalows. The climb concludes beyond
the houses, where the road ends and a
track begins.

TODHOLES HILL SANQUHAR

Distance 3.3 miles/5.3km
Total Height Gain 1017ft/310m
Altitude Range 463-1480ft/141-451m
Average Gradient 5.8%
Start B740/unclassified road junction, north of Sanquhar (NS 775110)
End Second road bend beyond cattle grid (NS 751147)
Map OS Landranger 71
Rail Sanquhar Station (1.1 mile)

A remarkably steady 1000ft climb towards the radio transmitter at the summit of Todholes Hill.

Leaving the B740, climb steadily on a very narrow road with central road markings, bound by a small wall on either side. This leads to a narrow bridge over the railway that is crossed with two sharp bends (right on approach, left after). Beyond, the road rises steadily on a straight stretch until it comes to a wide, sweep to the right which brings a change of direction. Further on, following a move to the left, two tight bends (right, then left) are negotiated before returning to a long, straight, steady climb up the hillside. At the end of this straight, a sharp bend to the right takes the road towards the first of a series of forested roadside areas.

The road sweeps broadly to the left as it reaches the forest, with a narrow strip beside the plantation which can be used for off-road parking. More significantly, there is a marked improvement in road quality at this point. Beyond the second pocket of trees, the road bends to the left and passes the track to Carcoside Farm, soon reaching another patch of forest to the left. Between these are expansive views down to the

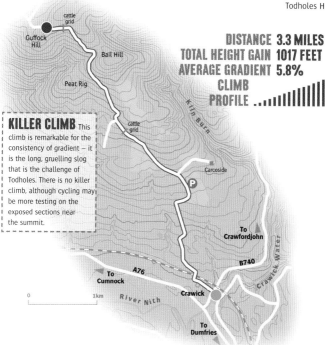

DISTANCE 3.3 MILES
TOTAL HEIGHT GAIN 1017 FEET
AVERAGE GRADIENT 5.8%
CLIMB
PROFILE

KILLER CLIMB This climb is remarkable for the consistency of gradient – it is the long, gruelling slog that is the challenge of Todholes. There is no killer climb, although cycling may be more testing on the exposed sections near the summit.

countryside below. Enjoy it while you can – the road is soon hemmed in by trees and hillside, sweeping to the left after passing a large roadside turning point at the forest edge, before emerging into open countryside after crossing a cattle grid at a break in the stone dyke.

Views open up once again and the summit can be seen in the distance. Surface quality deteriorates on a borderless road through rough grassland. The road swings to the right, then left to avoid losing height as it passes over a burn. After crossing, it rises

steadily up the side of Bail Hill where, from the lower part of the spur, there is a more marked change of direction (right, then left) to avoid dropping down into a narrow river valley. From above the gully, the road climbs with small bends to traverse the hillside above a second valley. Veering sharply to the left at this point, the road straightens and crosses the upper cattle grid at a break in the stone dyke. The summit is reached at the second bend beyond the cattle grid.

MENNOCK PASS AND GLENGONNAR HALT NITHSDALE

Distance 7.2 miles/11.5km
Total Height Gain 1237ft/377m
Altitude Range 423-1529ft/129-466m
Average Gradient 3.3%
Start A76/B797 junction at Mennock, southeast of Sanquhar (NS 873130)
End Cattle grid in Wanlockhead (NS 880135)
Map OS Landranger 78
Rail Sanquhar Station (2.6 miles)

This climb of over 1000 feet to Scotland's highest village is one that is likely to be familiar to followers of the Tour of Britain.

Join the B797 at Mennock and climb to a 90° turn over the railway bridge to start the ascent proper. The road rises stiffly, weaving up to a col before dropping more gently to join the valley through which the Mennock

Water flows, losing some but not all of the initial height gained. The descent comes to an end on reaching the second of the two tracks that peel away to the left.

The road now undulates as it weaves its way along the valley floor, heading east as it swings to the right at the second track junction, then north beyond a stone bridge. There are fewer undulations after a second stone bridge.

After crossing a cattle grid just beyond a small plantation, there is a change in landscape, now without roadside tree cover. The hills bank steeply to the left while to the right, alongside the river, the valley floor is more open. The incline remains gentle, with long straights interspersing three wide sweeping bends (left, right, left). After a staged, broad, sweeping bend to the

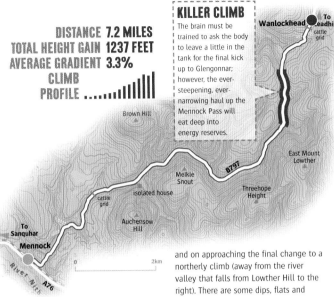

DISTANCE 7.2 MILES
TOTAL HEIGHT GAIN 1237 FEET
AVERAGE GRADIENT 3.3%
CLIMB PROFILE ......

KILLER CLIMB

The brain must be trained to ask the body to leave a little in the tank for the final kick up to Glengonnar; however, the ever-steepening, ever-narrowing haul up the Mennock Pass will eat deep into energy reserves.

To Wanlockhead Leadhills

cattle grid

Brown Hill

B797

East Mount Lowther

Meikle Snout

Threehope Height

cattle grid

isolated house

Auchensow Hill

To Sanquhar

Mennock

River Nith

A76

0   2km

right, the road emerges into a wide space dotted with antiquities and used for picnics and camping.

Crossing the bridge at the far end, the incline picks up significantly. From here to the summit of the Mennock Pass, the road hugs the side of the Mennock Water, sweeping around the foot of Middle Moor and Black Hill as it changes direction in four stages. The river valley continues to narrow as height is gained, although there is open aspect to the right between the first and second changes of direction (on rounding the lower spur of Middle Moor)

and on approaching the final change to a northerly climb (away from the river valley that falls from Lowther Hill to the right). There are some dips, flats and stretches of improved road, but on the whole this section makes for a stiff and steady challenge which follows a series of tight bends.

Wanlockhead soon presents itself on the descent from the col. Skirting the upper edge of the village, the road undulates on approach to a more marked dip as it veers right, before sweeping to the left for a return to tough climbing past a distinctive white house. The gradient then eases as it bends sharply to the right. On passing the turn-off to Lowther Hill, there is a final short haul up to the summit at the cattle grid.

LOWTHER HILL WANLOCKHEAD

Distance 2.9 miles/4.67km
Total Height Gain 1152ft/351m
Altitude Range 1280-2379ft/390-725m
Average Gradient 7.6%
Start Path/road junction in Wanlockhead (NS 873129)
End Summit of Lowther Hill (NS 890108)
Map OS Landranger 78
Rail Sanquhar Station (9.1 miles)

A taxing climb to the summit of Lowther Hill, largely on a private road belonging to National Air Traffic Services.

From Wanlockhead's Hidden Treasures museum, climb gently toward the right-hand switchback turn, from which the road rises steeply away. On reaching Goldscaur Row the gradient eases, picking up again at Lotus Lodge. The road narrows at two tight bends, before topping out soon after open aspect is reached. A short dip and a longer flat provide respite on approach to the road junction, reached after a short incline.

Turn left, then right to approach the road barrier at the fire station, and prepare to dismount. From here, the route to the summit is on a smooth twin-track road. Climb steeply, soon passing over a drain that traverses the road. The road weaves its way up along the route of a dry river valley, which is left behind as the road sweeps to the right through bog.

Now rising steadily in a southerly direction, there are clear views of the summit ridge. The road flattens momentarily on approach to the foot of a very steep incline, which starts and finishes at large parking/passing places. Beyond, the road rises more gently before levelling off and giving way to a short downhill as it curves to the right.

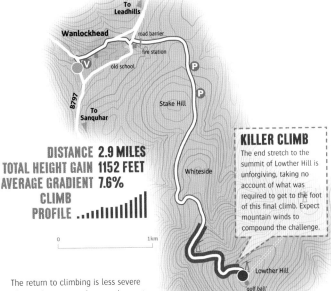

KILLER CLIMB

The end stretch to the summit of Lowther Hill is unforgiving, taking no account of what was required to get to the foot of this final climb. Expect mountain winds to compound the challenge.

DISTANCE 2.9 MILES
TOTAL HEIGHT GAIN 1152 FEET
AVERAGE GRADIENT 7.6%
CLIMB
PROFILE ....ıllıllIIIIıl

The return to climbing is less severe as the road cuts up and across the western slopes of Whiteside. Further on, it drops as it bends to the left before flattening on approach to the crossing of a river valley. The road rises steeply as it bends to the right at the crossing, this taxing climb continuing both on the straight that follows and around the wide sweep to the left that lies beyond.

A short straight after this bend precedes a curve to the right to join the northwest spur of Lowther Hill. A flat, then a dip brings the road to the foot of the spur proper. Rounding a right-hand bend, the steep ascent resumes, as before up a long straight, and continuing around a wide, sweeping bend to the left. The severity of

the climb eases on passing the transmitter, but returns thereafter.

On this final winding ascent, the Southern Upland Way path is crossed three times. Two gentler bends are encountered, before negotiating a 90° turn to the right. The steep climb continues on a staged left-hand bend. On a broad sweep to the right, this steepens further before winding up to reach the cattle grid and then continuing less severely to the road junction at the summit. The higher summit of Green Lowther is 1.1 miles beyond, but this returns a mere 8m net height gain and half a mile is spent travelling downhill.

Although Scotland's Border Country has its rocky coastlines, lowlying valleys and high agricultural plains, its most characteristic landscape feature is its seemingly never-ending rolling moorland hills and uplands. It should come as no surprise that the area has much to excite the road hillclimber. Indeed, the Scottish Borders has much more to offer the cyclist than can be presented in these few pages.

There is no space to describe the challenges of Wauchope and Whitrope, or the ascents from the west and east to Lauder Common, the three climbs around the iconic Eildon Hills to the roadside summit at Bowden Moor, or the ascent of Lamberton Moor from near Berwick-upon-Tweed. What is described here is a long climb away from Duns into the remote heart of the Lammermuir Hills, the ascent of the twin peaks of Burrowstown Moss in the bleak moorlands between Newcastleton and Langholm, a sinew-straining short climb away from Talla Reservoir and a dramatic rise away from

the North Sea at Pease Bay. The relative merits and inclusion in this volume of each of these climbs will no doubt stimulate much debate among those familiar with Borders cycling. However, there can be no doubt that the climb to the Scottish/English border at Carter's Bar would feature in any collection of road hillclimbs in Scotland's Border Country.

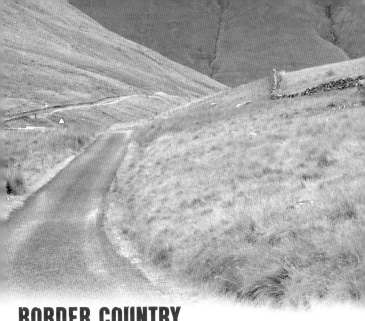

BORDER COUNTRY

TALLA LINN NORTHEAST OF MOFFAT

Distance 1.1 miles/1.7km
Total Height Gain 499ft/152m
Altitude Range 984-1483ft/300-452m
Average Gradient 8.4%
Start Warning sign on unclassified Talla Reservoir road (NT 135203)
End Cattle grid at milestone (NT 149202)
Map OS Landranger 72
Rail Lanark Station (30.1 miles), Lockerbie Station (35.7 miles)

A short, sharp shock of a climb, with momentary respite at the bridge crossing which divides its upper and lower sections.

This climb starts halfway along the minor road that joins the A701 at Tweedsmuir and the A708 at St Mary's Loch. The roadsign at the start of the climb forewarning of the 20% gradient that lies ahead is unnecessary, as the incline up the head of the valley towards the Megget Stone is clear for all to see from the eastern side of Talla Reservoir. From the outset, the road is narrow with both sides bordered by low walls. It is also very steep, making it difficult to find the energy to look back and enjoy the views of Talla Reservoir that fill the valley floor below.

Rising away from the roadsign, the direction of travel is immediately reversed as the road leaves behind the course of the Games Hope Burn to climb steeply up and across the northwest spur of Carlavin Hill.

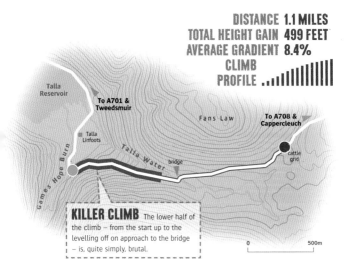

DISTANCE 1.1 MILES
TOTAL HEIGHT GAIN 499 FEET
AVERAGE GRADIENT 8.4%
CLIMB
PROFILE

Talla
Reservoir

To A701 &
Tweedsmuir

Talla
Linfoots

Games Hope Burn

Talla Water

bridge

Fans Law

To A708 &
Capercleuch

cattle
grid

KILLER CLIMB The lower half of
the climb – from the start up to the
levelling off on approach to the bridge
– is, quite simply, brutal.

0   500m

There are 14 bends to be negotiated before
you reach the bridge at the midpoint of the
climb. Despite the severity of the gradient,
these bends are gentle sweeps rather than
the switchbacks that may have been
expected. In the lower half, the first five
bends are tightly spaced, though the
straights between the bends lengthen as
the climb progresses. Despite the many
twists and the walled border, forward vision
is clear. The gradient levels out
momentarily on approach to the bridge
over the river.

The bridge is crossed with a swing to
the left on approach and the right on exit.
With two-thirds of the ascent completed
by this point, it's just one, final push to
the summit. On crossing the bridge,

it is well worth glancing to the left to
take in the view of the valley you have
left behind.

Overall, the second section of the ascent
is less steep, although the climb away from
the bridge is stiff. The gradient lessens at
the point at which the wall approaches the
road on your left-hand side. A long straight
now follows at a gentler gradient and
remains so until there is a change of
direction, following a series of sweeping
bends to the left. Now approaching the col
at the valley head, forward vision becomes
more limited as a series of tight bends are
negotiated on approach to the final
straight. The distinctive summit is reached
on crossing the cattle grid beside the
Megget Stone milestone.

BURROWSTOWN MOSS LANGHOLM

Distance 5.2 miles/8.3km
Total Height Gain 1165ft/355m
Altitude Range 282-1115ft/86-340m
Average Gradient 4.3%
Start A7/unclassified road junction north of Langholm (NY 366854)
End Cattle grid (NY 425872)
Map OS Landranger 79
Rail Lockerbie Station (18 miles)

A long climb across Border hill country that involves two significant climbs with a long descent of almost two miles in between.

The climb to Burrowstown Moss is most brutal at the outset. Leave the A7 north of Langholm to climb steeply up the hillside on two straights, separated by a right-hand bend, with views of the valley floor over the recently felled area. After a switchback to the left, the gradient eases, but remains stiff for the length of the straight to the sharp right-hand bend at a house.

Passing through farmland, the road continues to rise. High hedgerows obscure vision along long straights, interrupted by wide sweeping bends, and the road is bordered by forest from beyond the right-hand bend until the next left-hand bend. As the road passes under overhead lines, it enters a more open upland landscape.

A steady climb to the col at Charlie's Moss ensues with several well-placed benches giving excellent views of the

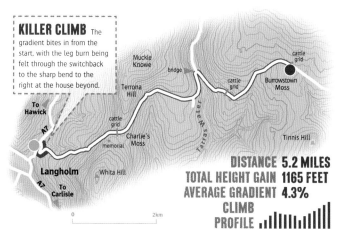

KILLER CLIMB The gradient bites in from the start, with the leg burn being felt through the switchback to the sharp bend to the right at the house beyond.

cattle grid

Muckle Knowe

bridge

cattle grid

Burrowstown Moss

Terrona Hill

To Hawick

A7

cattle grid

Charlie's Moss

memorial

Tarras Water

Tinnis Hill

Langholm

Whita Hill

A7

To Carlisle

0   2km

DISTANCE 5.2 MILES
TOTAL HEIGHT GAIN 1165 FEET
AVERAGE GRADIENT 4.3%
CLIMB PROFILE

surrounding hills. Lower down, the steady ascent is broken by a series of sharp turns to cross a burn, with a more marked climb away from the water. Further up, there is a more significant bend to the right before the roadside memorial and track junction. Now on the col, the road tops out on crossing a cattle grid.

From here, the road bends to the left to begin a gradual descent down the eastern side of Terrona Hill toward the tributaries of the Little Tarras Water. Two of these burns are crossed, with sharper bends to traverse the first. Beyond, the gentle climb resumes as the road cuts across the plateau above Middlemoss Head, before starting to drop. The rate of descent increases after the track down to Middlemoss Farm, sweeping to the left and dropping steeply on a straight to cross the

Tarras Water, with sharp rights immediately before and after the crossing.

The approach to Burrowstown Moss begins with a steep ascent up and away from the river valley. Visibility is hampered on approach to the sharp bend to the left, beyond which there are less significant bends and a cattle grid. After a short straight, there are a few bends and dips to negotiate some minor burns. A marked change of direction at a left-hand bend denotes a return to steady climbing. There's another left-hand bend as the road follows the course of the river valley, with more bends further on to the right and left. On crossing the Black Grain, the road veers to the right, the gradient eases and the summit is soon reached at the cattle grid where the roadsign welcomes travellers to the Scottish Borders.

CARTER'S BAR SOUTH OF JEDBURGH

Distance 5.1 miles/8.25km
Total Height Gain 1027ft/313m
Altitude Range 420-1371ft/128-418m
Average Gradient 3.8%
Start Bridge over Jed Water on A86 at
Camptown (NT 679136)
End The border (NT 698068)
Map OS Landranger 80
Rail Berwick Station (40.5 miles), Gretna
Station (55.1 miles)

**The wide, open switchbacks with
expansive views of the Cheviot Hills on
approach to the summit Border crossing
make this a worthy addition to southern
Scotland's best road hillclimbs.**

Beyond the bridge on the A86 at
Camptown, south of Jedburgh, climb
steadily past the cottages and up the
valley side. A gentle kink to the right is
followed by a sharper bend to the left,
where the road steepens further. Now
enclosed by trees on either side, the crash
barrier is a reminder of the need to keep on
the road. Leaving the forest behind after
four short bends, the initial climb tops out
in open farmland.

Here, the middle section of the climb
begins, rising and falling for 1.5 miles to
reach the base of the final ascent to
Carter's Bar. A straight takes the road down
to a parking place, then up to briefly enter
forest once more. Tree cover on the left
ends at a right-hand bend and a short
straight rises to top out at Home Farm,
with views to the surrounding hills opening
up immediately to the left.

After a short dip and a sweeping bend to
the left, past the parking area, climbing
resumes. A gentle ascent tops out at a wide
right-hand bend beyond enclosed forest.
The road descends for a third time at a
broad sweep, passing another parking place,
this time to the left. It is a staged
descent, dropping more

SCOTLAND

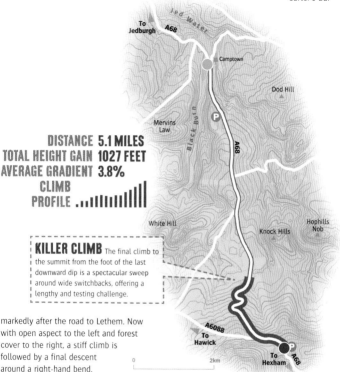

DISTANCE 5.1 MILES
TOTAL HEIGHT GAIN 1027 FEET
AVERAGE GRADIENT 3.8%
CLIMB
PROFILE ....ıllıllılllllll

KILLER CLIMB The final climb to the summit from the foot of the last downward dip is a spectacular sweep around wide switchbacks, offering a lengthy and testing challenge.

markedly after the road to Lethem. Now with open aspect to the left and forest cover to the right, a stiff climb is followed by a final descent around a right-hand bend.

The steady climb to the summit is memorable, with a wide, sweeping curve to the right beyond an initial short, straight climb away from the dip; this leads to the foot of the first of three broad switchback bends (left, right, left), each with crash barriers lending dramatic effect.

Beyond the last switchback, the road bends to the right and continues its steady ascent up to and beyond a left-hand bend to reach a road junction, at which you have right of way. The climb steepens around the right-hand bend on approach to the summit, which can be busy with tourists in summer. The summit should be approached via the slip road to the parking area. A distinctive viewpoint at the milestone marks the border.

HARDENS AND MAINSLAUGHTER DUNS

Distance 8.9 miles/14.3km
Total Height Gain 1493ft/455m
Altitude Range 400-1358ft/122-414m
Average Gradient 3.2%
Start A6105/unclassified road junction just west of Duns, Berwickshire (NT 772532)
End Summit bend beyond cattle grid on Mainslaughter Law (NT 661603)
Maps OS Landranger 74 and 67
Rail Berwick Station (15.4 miles)

Two peaks and two smaller tops are traversed on a memorable route on good-quality roads with little traffic.

From the junction of the A6105 west of Duns and the minor Longformacus road, the climb starts unremarkably, following a series of long straights, initially with gentle inclines. The short straight before the first left-hand bend is followed by two longer straights, separated by a right-hand bend. At the left-hand bend beyond, the road steepens and is bordered by a broken line of trees.

The character of the climb changes at the next left-hand bend. Much shorter straights are interspersed with bends as the road climbs steeply up Hardens Hill on a route used in local hillclimbing races. Further on, the straights lengthen and, from a right-hand bend, the incline is more gentle, weaving its way to summit in open countryside after the Langtonless farm road.

Now for the descent over open hill – at first gentle, on straights interrupted by bends. The descent steepens after the last of these bends. Sharper bends to the left, then right reorient the road, before it drops steeply to a sharp right-hand bend where it is joined by a thin belt of trees. From here,

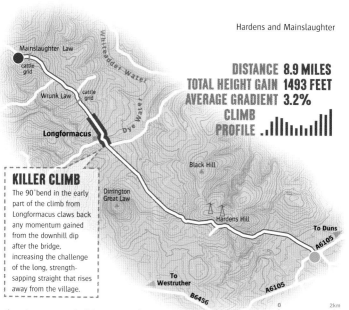

DISTANCE 8.9 MILES
TOTAL HEIGHT GAIN 1493 FEET
AVERAGE GRADIENT 3.2%
CLIMB PROFILE

KILLER CLIMB

The 90° bend in the early part of the climb from Longformacus claws back any momentum gained from the downhill dip after the bridge, increasing the challenge of the long, strength-sapping straight that rises away from the village.

there is a more gradual descent on a long straight broken by a right-hand bend, with a more marked drop to cross the Kippetlaw Burn towards the end.

A steep ascent from the bridge soon eases to a steady climb on a long straight, sheltered on either side by a narrow band of trees. From the high point, a gentle descent gives way to a steep drop through tight bends to the village of Longformacus, swerving sharply left to cross the Dye Water.

The climb away from the river is particularly steep, initially veering left. The severity of the incline eases after a 90° right-hand bend, which is followed by a wider sweeping bend to the left, where the road steepens again. As it straightens, it continues to climb stiffly away from the

village, sheltered by a band of trees.

Towards the end of the tree cover, the road dips briefly. The ascent of Wrunk Law begins gently, but stiffens on approach to and beyond the cattle grid, easing off again after reaching the road to Redpath Farm. The indistinct road summit of Wrunk Law is reached a few bends further on.

After a left-hand bend, there is a short descent to the road junction, before a swift start to the final climb up the spur. As it follows the spur, the road bends to the right, then in steeper steps to the left on approach to the road summit on Mainslaughter Law. This is reached at the sharp right-hand bend beyond the cattle grid.

PEASE BAY NORTH OF ST ABBS

Distance 3.1 miles/5km
Total Height Gain 722ft/220m
Altitude Range 26-745ft/8-227m
Average Gradient 4.4%
Start Bridge/ford at Pease Bay (NT 794707)
End By distinctive gorse bush (NT 831687)
Map OS Landranger 67
Rail Dunbar Station (9.6 miles)

The initial climb is viciously steep, rising up a gully that cuts through the cliff face, and is followed by a long drawn-out climb up and across the hillside to summit on Penmanshiel Moor. There are panoramic seascape views in the early stages of the climb.

Cross the ford at the Pease Bay Leisure Park, where a sign states that the climb to be tackled is 'unsuited for caravans'. It soon becomes apparent why, as the gradient stiffens quickly and remains taxing up through the dry valley that breaks up the sea cliffs. A series of right-hand bends are interspersed with short straights on a narrow road of excellent quality. The road emerges at the top, takes a sharp left-hand bend and becomes markedly less severe after reaching the gate in the stone wall.

Given the early exertions, the much gentler climb will now seem like respite. Turn right at the road junction, with right of way, to climb steadily through gently sloping farmland. Road quality is good, although there is a wide, rough border on either side. The road flattens on passing a large parking/passing place.

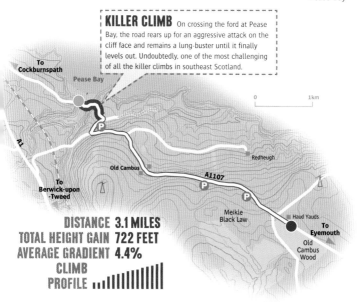

KILLER CLIMB On crossing the ford at Pease Bay, the road rears up for an aggressive attack on the cliff face and remains a lung-buster until it finally levels out. Undoubtedly, one of the most challenging of all the killer climbs in southeast Scotland.

DISTANCE 3.1 MILES
TOTAL HEIGHT GAIN 722 FEET
AVERAGE GRADIENT 4.4%
CLIMB PROFILE

An opportunity should be taken on the level to look ahead for fine views of Fife and Bass Rock in the distance. At the end of the parking place, after passing under the telegraph poles, the road rises up to join the A1107.

Turn left. Although there are a number of kinks in the road, the remainder of this ascent comprises a series of straights which afford good forward vision. From the junction, the gradient steepens, although not as markedly as the initial climb away from the coast.

The gradient eases on approach to the minor road junction for Redheugh Farm. At this point, the A1107 swings to the right, changing direction on a now imperceptible climb toward the hamlet of Old Cambus. Swinging widely to the left to change direction once more at Old Cambus, there is a return to climbing. The steady and straight ascent up the hillside passes a parking place/viewpoint and a narrow bank of trees, before swinging to the right on approach to the final climb, past a second parking place. The gradient picks up a little after a left-hand bend, returning to a gentle incline beyond the minor road junction. Continue ahead on the A1107 to summit beside the distinctive gorse bush in the field to the left shortly after the stone building.

Hills are synonymous with the city of Edinburgh. The city centre skyline is dominated by Arthur's Seat and Edinburgh Castle atop their volcanic plugs. Every summer, there is a road/trail race around the 'seven hills of Edinburgh' and each lunchtime a collection of runners and cyclists of all abilities work their way steadily around the road that circumnavigates Holyrood Park. The road around Arthur's Seat may not be the toughest challenge in the south of Scotland, but it does have the unique advantage of being a true city centre road climb, which affords unparalleled views of Scotland's capital. Bordered to the north and east by the Firth of Forth, road hillclimbing beyond the city requires venturing further afield to the south and west. To the west, the hills known to local club cyclists as the Bathgate Alps offer a multitude of hillclimb challenges. The climb featured in this chapter brings together five mini-climbs in one gargantuan challenge. To the south, the escarpments of the Moorfoot and Lammermuir Hills provide many opportunities for longer climbs, with Bransly Hill, White Castle and The Granites making for memorable challenges.

AROUND EDINBURGH

BRANSLY HILL DUNBAR

Distance 4.3 miles/6.85km
Total Height Gain 1096ft/334m
Altitude Range 131-1148ft/40-350m
Average Gradient 4.8%
Start A1/unclassified road junction five miles southeast of Dunbar (NT 719750)
End Cattle grid (NT 685698)
Map OS Landranger 67
Rail Dunbar Station (3.6 miles)

A steady incline to the foot of the escarpment of the Lammermuir Hills concludes with a stiff climb up to the summit plateau.

Climb steeply away from the A1 on the road for Thurston Manor, bending to the left. The incline softens on the wide sweeping bend to the right that follows, continuing on the straight beyond and through another left-hand bend. A momentary levelling on a straight precedes a sharper left-hand bend

and a return to stiffer climbing, topping out a short distance beyond Thurston Manor Leisure Park. A brief dip to the cemetery turn-off is followed by a stiff climb into a forest-enclosed road, bending to the right. Emerging into open countryside, continue ahead, ignoring the road to Woodhall.

The climb tops out a short distance beyond the junction. With tree cover to the left and farmland to the right, the road is now clearly single track. A flat section follows, negotiating a sharp Z-bend (right, then left), before following a straight and a gentler Z-bend (right, then left) to reach the foot of a short incline. Thereafter, a short dip brings the road to another junction. Ignore Aikengall and veer right. A gentle climb through a chicane (left, right, left) continues on a long straight. At the end of the straight, the road bends to the left and drops down in three stages (steeper, gentler,

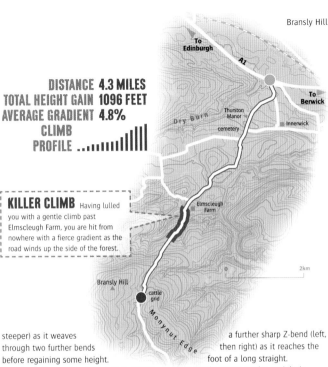

Bransly Hill

To Edinburgh

A1

To Berwick

DISTANCE 4.3 MILES
TOTAL HEIGHT GAIN 1096 FEET
AVERAGE GRADIENT 4.8%
CLIMB
PROFILE illl

Dry Burn

Thurston Manor

cemetery

Innerwick

KILLER CLIMB Having lulled you with a gentle climb past Elmscleugh Farm, you are hit from nowhere with a fierce gradient as the road winds up the side of the forest.

Elmscleugh Farm

2km

Bransly Hill

cattle grid

Monynut Edge

steeper) as it weaves through two further bends before regaining some height.

From here, the road undulates as it mirrors the course of the Elmscleugh Water until it meets the road for Woodhall/Brunt.

Continue ahead to soon pass Elmscleugh Farm on a particularly rough section of road. Beyond, climb steeply away from the sharp left-hand bend and, after a sharp right-hand bend, follow the line of plantation trees. Road quality improves as height is gained. After a gentle swing to the right, and a sharper Z-bend (left, then right), the road peels right to move away from the forest side. The severity of the climb eases beyond

a further sharp Z-bend (left, then right) as it reaches the foot of a long straight.

The steady ascent up the straight is followed by a gentle sweep to the right and then two sharper bends (left, then right) as the road reorients itself for a steep and direct climb up the hillside. A false summit is passed a short distance beyond the track junction. The undulations after this lower summit end with a sharp dip to cross a burn. Bending sharp right beyond the dip, the road then curves to the right on a steady climb toward the higher summit. The final few yards to the cattle grid at the summit are on rougher road.

WHITE CASTLE GARVALD

Distance 2.65 miles/4km
Total Height Gain 817ft/249m
Altitude Range 420-1132ft/128-345m
Average Gradient 5.8%
Start Bridge in Garvald (NT 589708)
End Indistinct point beyond road bend
(NT 616683)
Map OS Landranger 67
Rail Dunbar Station (10 miles), Drem
Station (10.5 miles)

A difficult route into the Lammermuir Hills combining three challenging main ascents with some testing descents along the way.

Turn sharp left after the bridge over the Sounding Burn in Garvald, East Lothian, to climb steeply up the side of the densely vegetated valley. This is the first of six bends which are negotiated as the road weaves its way up to emerge from forest at the distinctive stone-arched gatehouse to Nunraw.

Now bordered by a high stone wall to the left and open farmland beyond hedgerow to the right, the road sweeps to the right and climbs steeply up to a 90° left-hand bend. Maintaining the same borders beyond the bend, a short, flat straight precedes a return to climbing, as the road once again sweeps gently to the right on a stiff ascent.

The road levels as it straightens on passing Nunraw Abbey. Two sharp 90° bends (left, then right) are passed on the level, before dropping steeply down to the valley floor. The road rises equally steeply to enter

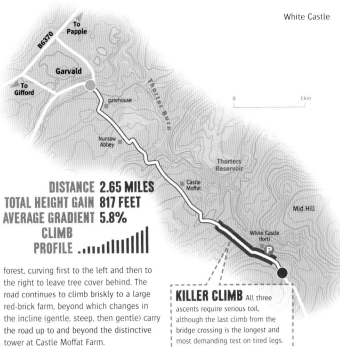

DISTANCE 2.65 MILES
TOTAL HEIGHT GAIN 817 FEET
AVERAGE GRADIENT 5.8%
CLIMB
PROFILE

KILLER CLIMB All three ascents require serious toil, although the last climb from the bridge crossing is the longest and most demanding test on tired legs.

forest, curving first to the left and then to the right to leave tree cover behind. The road continues to climb briskly to a large red-brick farm, beyond which changes in the incline (gentle, steep, then gentle) carry the road up to and beyond the distinctive tower at Castle Moffat Farm.

Surrounded briefly by trees on both sides, from here to the summit the road is more clearly single track. Another dip brings you to a left-hand bend and, after a brief return to climbing, a third descent starts as the road arcs to the right, dropping sharply – with crash barriers for comfort – to bottom out at a left-hand bend. Now in a distinctly upland landscape, there's a short, sharp rise over a spur, dropping down to cross a burn on the other side.

The stiff climb away from the final dip starts on a bend to the right, shortly followed by one to the left as the road skirts the side of an old quarry. The gradient eases, then picks up on the straight beyond, climbing directly toward the upper hill slope. On the hillside, the ascent is also steep and direct, although it is broken by two gentle bends, then two sharper bends, before a short, flat straight takes the road more gradually up to the far end of the parking area at White Castle fort. The stiff climb away from the parking place eases at a right-hand bend and the road tops out a little way beyond the next left-hand bend.

THE GRANITES NEWBATTLE

Distance 9.5 miles/15.2km
Total Height Gain 1227ft/374m
Altitude Range 148-1312ft/45-400m
Average Gradient 2.5%
Start B703 bridge over the River South Esk in Newbattle (NT 331657)
End County boundary (NT 348533)
Map OS Landranger 66
Rail Musselburgh Station (5.9 miles), Edinburgh Waverley Station (7.3 miles)

A very steady climb from the plains of East Lothian into the Moorfoot Hills. The views from near the summit extend on a clear day to the Pentlands and Fife.

Soon after crossing the bridge over the River South Esk, the road starts to climb stiffly through four bends. On passing the road junction beyond the final right-hand bend, the incline eases for a short straight, the steep ascent resuming up to the old church on the outskirts of Newtongrange. Continue ahead in the direction of Gorebridge, passing through a double roundabout and over three raised pedestrian crossing points as you climb gently through Newtongrange.

On reaching the wheel at the far end of the town, turn left for a steeper climb on the A7. The incline eases soon after passing the Scottish Mining Museum, this steadier climb persisting until just after the petrol station, before the traffic lights at the B704 junction. Continue ahead. A long, steady descent to the bridge over the Gore Glen starts at the Dewar Park housing development, dropping more steeply beyond the Kirkhill Mansion B&B.

Climb steeply at the left-hand bend beyond the bridge, easing to a steady ascent from the next right-hand bend approaching the junction with the B6372 to Penicuik at the far end of Gorebridge. Continue ahead. Once more, the road dips,

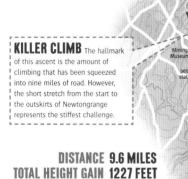

KILLER CLIMB The hallmark of this ascent is the amount of climbing that has been squeezed into nine miles of road. However, the short stretch from the start to the outskirts of Newtongrange represents the stiffest challenge.

DISTANCE 9.6 MILES
TOTAL HEIGHT GAIN 1227 FEET
AVERAGE GRADIENT 2.5%
CLIMB PROFILE ......ıılIllI

at first slightly and then, from the cemetery, more steeply, down to the minor road junction to Catcune. The steady, rising gradient returns, steepening as the road curves to the left beyond the works depot for a two-lane climb. This pattern is repeated with a drop to the crossroads for Borthwick/North Middleton, followed by a sweep to the left as the road stiffens in a two-lane climb, before straightening and rising more directly up the hillside.

Turn right off the A7 to join the B7007 in the direction of Innerleithen, leaving behind heavy traffic. Aspect improves significantly at the end of the stone wall and forward vision is good on this long, straight stretch of road. Soon, the final climb up the hillside of Broad Law can be viewed ahead. After a wide, sweeping bend to the right, the

incline steepens markedly and a long, steady ascent up and across the hillside commences. Now views begin to open up ahead towards the Pentland Hills and to the right toward Fife and the Lothians. The summit is reached beyond a final left-hand bend, leading to the roadsign marking the start of the Scottish Borders.

ARTHUR'S SEAT EDINBURGH

Distance 1.6 miles/2.6km
Total Height Gain 266ft/81m
Altitude Range 121-387ft/37-118m
Average Gradient 3.1%
Start Unclassified road junction at Duke's Walk/Queen's Drive (NT 277740)
End Bend at summit (NT 274726)
Map OS Landranger 66
Rail Edinburgh Waverley Station (1.4 miles)

A city hillclimb! This unique road, much used by runners and cyclists, works its way around the largest of the seven hills of Edinburgh and gives outstanding views of the city and further afield to East Lothian, West Lothian and Fife.

From the red gates at the Duke's Walk in Holyrood Park, the climb around Arthur's Seat starts with a bend to the left on the smooth surfaced single-track Queen's Drive, bound to the right by a gorse-clad bank and to the left by a tree-covered slope.

After a short distance, the road veers to the right. The view opens to the hillside above after the first of several parking places and, though this is concealed by steep banking after a further bend to the right, there is no sense of being enclosed on this long stretch of road which has only the most minor of twists and turns. The steady gradient of the lower half of the climb becomes more marked at the second bend beyond the second parking place. A short section of steeper climbing carries the road around to the right and ends soon after the third parking place. From here, views open up to the left toward East Lothian and to the right toward Arthur's Seat. The gradient is now much less marked on

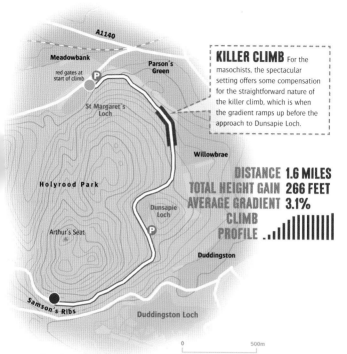

KILLER CLIMB For the masochists, the spectacular setting offers some compensation for the straightforward nature of the killer climb, which is when the gradient ramps up before the approach to Dunsapie Loch.

DISTANCE 1.6 MILES
TOTAL HEIGHT GAIN 266 FEET
AVERAGE GRADIENT 3.1%
CLIMB PROFILE

0   500m

approach to the 90° bend to the right that redirects the road toward Dunsapie Loch.

Leaving the East Lothian views behind at the bend, it is possible to catch a glimpse back towards Fife on a clear day. There is a picturesque hillscape ahead as the road gently winds its way around Dunsapie Loch, passing several parking places and a larger off-road car park. At the far end of the loch, the road changes direction, bending to the right, with a return to city views of south

Edinburgh and East Lothian. The road is now twin track and affords excellent forward vision with expansive views stretching as far as the Pentlands. Further along, the gradient picks up slightly from the bend on approach to the summit, which is reached in the cutting between the outcrop to the left and the upper slopes of Arthur's Seat to the right. From the summit, there are uninterrupted views ahead to Edinburgh Castle.

BATHGATE ALPS QUINTET LINLITHGOW

Distance 4.3 miles/6.9km
Total Height Gain 1017ft/310m
Altitude Range 187-955ft/57-291m
Average Gradient 4.5%
Start Under railway bridge on Linlithgow's
Preston Road (NS 996770)
End Brow of hill on The Knock (NS 991712)
Map OS Landranger 65
Rail Linlithgow Station (0.6 miles)

**A long climb of almost 1000ft, rising
from Linlithgow, an ancient seat of
Scottish royalty, to beyond Cairnpapple
Hill, a major prehistoric site.**

Preston Road rises from Linlithgow's West
Port up to Beecraigs Country Park. From
under the railway bridge at the start, a sign
advises of 1050 yards of traffic calming.
This comprises five broken bumps, which
can be cycled between, and five cross-road
stretches of raised pathway, negotiated on a

straight concave slope, which is reached as
the road sweeps to the left, having climbed
away from the bridge. The road levels out
as it passes Donaldson's School.

In open countryside, the road narrows,
enclosed by a stone wall. A steep ascent
awaits after a brief drop and an approach
climb of three steps, beginning with a sharp
bend of almost 90° to the left. Now with
high hedges to both sides, the gradient
remains stiff. A switchback to the right is
followed by two gentler bends to the left,
after which the road rises directly up the
hillside, bordered by a belt of forest. Beyond
the trees, the climb from Preston Road tops
out. Continue ahead, then branch left to join
the minor road for Balvormie and Wardlaw.

Now in forest on a single-track road, a
gentle downhill past an adventure
playground and car park precedes a climb as

DISTANCE **4.3 MILES**
TOTAL HEIGHT GAIN **1017 FEET**
AVERAGE GRADIENT **4.5%**
CLIMB
PROFILE ..ıılıllıllıl

the road bends to the left, then right before straightening and descending to the foot of a straight. The stepped ascent that follows is known locally as the Wall of Wairdlaw, an ever-steepening concave slope which tops out after the forest. Two bends are followed by a straight, steep descent with a sharp bend to the right at the bottom.

Climbing steeply away, the road curves gently to the right and then more markedly to the left, steepening further on the second bend. The gradient eases on reaching forest. From the brow of the hill, the summit of the Mains Burn climb, the road dips down through the trees to a road junction with open farmland ahead.

Turn right, to soon re-enter forest. Starting with two gentle descents broken by a gentle incline, this section concludes with a steady climb, which continues into open countryside on approach to a final road junction. Turn left here.

The climb is stiff after the junction, easing at the end of the crash barriers as the road bends to the right. Sweeping to the left to pass the Cairnpapple parking area, the summit of this climb of the same name, the road veers to the right and begins to descend – on a straight after some initial bends. A sharp left turn at the valley floor is

KILLER CLIMB

The final ascent, starting with a wicked bend at the valley floor, has a 1:6 gradient that will have your lungs screaming for mercy.

followed by a very stiff climb up and across the hillside, with crash barriers to the left. The gradient lessens on approach to the road summit of The Knock, which is reached on the brow of the hill, just before a minor road branching off to the left.

The Central Lowlands, or Midland Valley, of Scotland is the low-lying band of land that sits between the Highland Boundary Fault to the north and the Southern Uplands Fault to the south. The name does not suggest a paradise for those seeking road hillclimbs. However, the area presents a range of hillclimbing challenges, many of which are widely known and celebrated among cyclists in Scotland.

Indeed, the low-lying plains that surround the escarpments and volcanic plugs of central Scotland lend emphasis to these climbs, setting them apart from the surrounding landscape in a much more dramatic fashion than in the higher lands to the north and south. East Lomond Hill is a prime example, rewarding the hillclimber

with uninterrupted views of the Firth of Forth and wider Fife area from the car park at the summit.

Sheriffmuir and Earl's Hill may be less known to those beyond Stirlingshire, but each is a testing climb that quickly removes the traveller from the urban fringe to what seems like remote countryside in a few hard-earned miles of ascent. Revered throughout Scotland by hillclimbers of the motorsport variety is the Doune Hill Climb. Although far from the most challenging of southern Scotland's climbs, the aura and quality of this traffic-free road is somewhat special. Finally, there is Duke's Pass, one of southern Scotland's best-known climbs, in the heart of the picturesque Trossachs and an integral part of the Tour de Trossachs Time Trial race.

84

CENTRAL LOWLANDS

PURIN DEN, EAST LOMOND HILL
FALKLAND

Distance 1.4 miles/2.3km
Total Height Gain 745ft/227m
Altitude Range 354-1099ft/108-335m
Average Gradient 10%
Start A912/unclassified road junction southeast of Falkland (NO 272061)
End Radio transmitter gates (NO 252059)
Map OS Landranger 58
Rail Ladybank Station (4.5 miles), Markinch Station (4.4 miles)

Scaling one of Fife's most celebrated landmarks makes for a memorable climb. From the summit, there are spectacular views of much of the Kingdom and the Firth of Forth.

Leave the A912 southeast of Falkland at the sign for East Lomond Hill. The route to the summit is on a quality single-track road with ample passing places and a steady gradient throughout. If the weather is good, the road is likely to be busy with cars heading to the viewpoint.

The climb starts with a series of four tight bends interspersed with very short straights on a road hemmed in by mature trees on either side. A transition is evident after the passing place across from a felled area which reveals a ravine nearby. From here, the straights are longer between bends and the roadside trees less dense, with glimpses of the rolling farmland beyond the stone

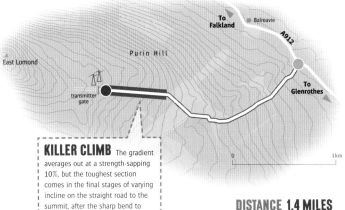

KILLER CLIMB
The gradient averages out at a strength-sapping 10%, but the toughest section comes in the final stages of varying incline on the straight road to the summit, after the sharp bend to the left.

DISTANCE 1.4 MILES
TOTAL HEIGHT GAIN 745 FEET
AVERAGE GRADIENT 10%
CLIMB
PROFILE ....

wall. Once more, there are four bends between straights.

Now the road sweeps right, changing the direction of travel from southwesterly to westerly. Plantation forest lines the right side of the road and, briefly, deciduous woodland the left until you reach a burn crossing on approach to a Z-bend.

After negotiating the Z-bend (right, then left), there is a short straight through open farmland and then plantation forest. A longer straight through the plantation follows a further bend to the right, now bearing northwest – the climb is characteristically steady on this straight. The forest ends shortly before a final bend to the left, which brings the road to the foot of the last ascent.

This final push is a straight quarter-mile in a westerly direction, passing through rough, open moorland. There are subtle changes in gradient – a steep section to start, followed very swiftly by a longer, gentler stretch, an equally long concave stretch, a flat step, a further concave stretch, a second flat step and a final short and steep leg-worker. However, none of these changes should be overstated, as the predominant character is that of a steady climb. This tops out at the radio transmitter gates at the entrance to the viewpoint car park.

SHERIFFMUIR EAST OF BRIDGE OF ALLAN

Distance 4.6 miles/7.4km
Total Height Gain 1155ft/352m
Altitude Range 43-1033ft/13-315m
Average Gradient 4.8%
Start B998/unclassified road junction east of the Stirling University campus (NS 818966)
End Road bend beyond Sheriffmuir Inn (NN 833026)
Map OS Landranger 57
Rail Bridge of Allan Station (3.3 miles), Stirling Station (2.75 miles)

The longest of four routes to the highest point of the road at Sheriffmuir, with panoramic views and an historic drovers' inn at the summit.

Leaving behind the car park, the climb sets out innocuously on a wide single-track road, but soon narrows and steepens for a stiff ascent, tightly hemmed in by high walls. From the start, the road sweeps to the left, then more sharply right, before straightening on approach to the Old Logie Kirk graveyard. The road steepens on passing the graveyard and even more so beyond it. After a brief section of tough climbing, a sharp switchback to the left is encountered. The ascent remains hard-going after the bend and steepens further after a sharp right bend, continuing so until it emerges from the trees. The road rises less severely from here, finally levelling out on approach to the T-junction.

Turn right to climb again, although not as stiffly as before. Leaving the forest behind, the road weaves around knolls with parking places, the gradient easing as it swings to the right. After passing beneath pylons, a dip carries the road down to the bridge at the foot of a band of open forest.

Climbing up along and beyond the trees, the road then dips down towards some part-

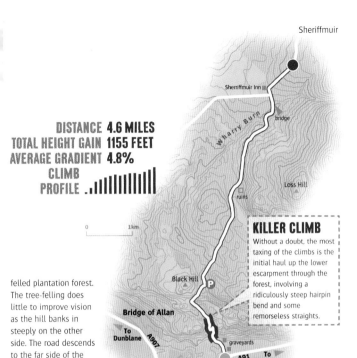

Sheriffmuir

Sherriffmuir Inn

bridge

Wharry Burn

Loss Hill

ruins

DISTANCE 4.6 MILES
TOTAL HEIGHT GAIN 1155 FEET
AVERAGE GRADIENT 4.8%
CLIMB PROFILE

Black Hill

P

Bridge of Allan

To Dunblane A907

graveyards

A91 **To Menstrie**

Stirling University

To Stirling A91

0   1km

KILLER CLIMB

Without a doubt, the most taxing of the climbs is the initial haul up the lower escarpment through the forest, involving a ridiculously steep hairpin bend and some remorseless straights.

felled plantation forest. The tree-felling does little to improve vision as the hill banks in steeply on the other side. The road descends to the far side of the plantation and flattens as it sweeps to the right, passing old ruined farm buildings.

The spur of Loss Hill is now tackled, with the road rising through a narrow band of plantation forest, before undulating and then passing through a second band of forest. From here, the road bypasses several small clumps of forest, continuing to undulate as it cuts across the hillside. A more marked downhill follows as the road swings down through a series of twists to the Wharry Bridge.

The road crosses the bridge and follows the course of the burn, before turning more steeply away to the left. The incline is fairly steep at the outset and continues to rise steadily toward the white Sheriffmuir Inn on the horizon. On passing the inn, the road sweeps sharply to the right for a steady climb on a straight but badly surfaced section. The summit is reached beyond the bend at the double gate with parking space.

EARL'S HILL STIRLING

Distance 5.2 miles/8.3km
Total Height Gain 1161ft/354m
Altitude Range 131-1129ft/40-344m
Average Gradient 4%
Start Minor road junction after bridge over the M9 (NS 784920)
End Road bend/fourth pole (NS 723879)
Map OS Landranger 57
Rail Stirling Station (1.6 miles)

A difficult climb which takes the rider from city outskirts to open countryside in a few short but steep miles. The challenge is compounded by very poor road quality in places.

Start at the roundabout by the more southern of the two bridges, over the M9, that connect Cambusbarron with Stirling. Leave the bridge to head up Polmaise Road. The gentle gradient of the initial wide, sweeping bend to the right picks up before steepening markedly along a forested section. Still rising beyond this point, there is a brief dip before the climb resumes up to the 90° bend at Graystale. A roadside bench hints that there are views back over Stirling and the Ochil Hills to be enjoyed from a sideways glance.

With right of way all yours, veer to the right and enjoy a long, staged descent. There's a sharp left-hand bend at the cementworks' entrance to continue the descent, bottoming out at the North Third Forest parking place.

Now, a long section of barely perceptible climbing with forest to the left is followed by a steep ascent of three steps, topping out at the activity area with hillside opening up on your right. From the top, the descent starts gently, but steepens after a

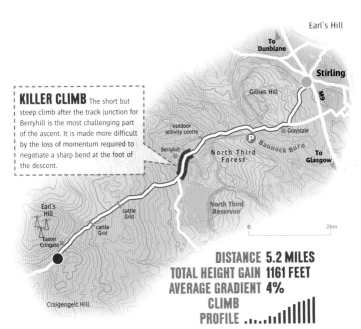

KILLER CLIMB The short but steep climb after the track junction for Berryhill is the most challenging part of the ascent. It is made more difficult by the loss of momentum required to negotiate a sharp bend at the foot of the descent.

DISTANCE 5.2 MILES
TOTAL HEIGHT GAIN 1161 FEET
AVERAGE GRADIENT 4%
CLIMB PROFILE

right-hand bend which leaves the forest cover. A gradual rise takes the road to a sharp left bend and the foot of another significant ascent – beyond the turn-off to Berryhill lies the convex killer climb which brings the road to Shielbrae.

Swing right at the fork after Shielbrae, rising steeply at the outset. Although open hillside soon makes for improved vision, pay attention to the road to avoid some very large potholes. The road climbs directly up the hillface in short, steep stages.

A subtle change in profile follows as, although the climbing persists, there are several pronounced dips between rises. Protection from the elements is afforded by

a stone wall on either side of the road, though this shelter is lost after chicaning over a bridge and cattle grid. From here, the climb is less taxing with fewer dips and longer, gentler straights up to the more marked descent to cross a second cattle grid and bridge.

The initial climb away from the bridge is on a very steep but uncharacteristically resurfaced road. The gradient eases as the ascent continues on the improved road up to the isolated house after the track junction for the top of Earl's Hill. From here, a rough surface takes the route to its summit at an indistinct road bend beside the fourth telegraph pole.

DOUNE HILL DOUNE

Distance 0.9 miles/1.5km
Total Height Gain 190ft/58m
Altitude Range 157-328ft/48-100m
Average Gradient 3.9%
Start Wooden bar across road, off the A84 on the edge of Doune (NN 716030)
End White finish lines (NN 717033)
Map OS Landranger 57
Rail Dunblane Station (5 miles)

Scotland's premier venue for motorsport hillclimbing provides a unique traffic-free experience on a road of impeccable quality. Note that this is not a public road.

The hillclimb course can be accessed off the Doune-Callander road by the Scottish Antiques & Arts Centre. The painted white line that marks the motorsport start point lies a little downhill from the wooden bar that straddles the road outside race days. Rising stiffly from the start, the road bends to the left beyond the bar, the gradient easing at the start of a wooden fence. Double crash barriers feature intermittently throughout the climb.

Skirting the bottom of the hill, the road follows five straights broken by four bends. The gradient picks up slightly midway through this lower section and, on the penultimate straight, a band of forest provides cover on the left-hand side.

On passing a viewing platform after the fifth straight, the road bends 90° to the right to commence a stiff and direct ascent of the hillside. To the right, open hill gives way to a thin band of forest cover and for a short time the road is enclosed. The steepest part of this stiff climb finishes in the enclosed section just before the end of the stone wall and the start of a crash barrier; it is marked by a concrete band across the road. Leaving the forest behind on the right, the route continues to rise,

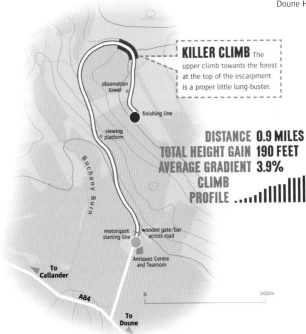

KILLER CLIMB The upper climb towards the forest at the top of the escarpment is a proper little lung-buster.

observation tower

finishing line

viewing platform

Buchany Burn

motorsport starting line

wooden gate/bar across road

Antiques Centre and Tearoom

To Callander

A84

To Doune

DISTANCE 0.9 MILES
TOTAL HEIGHT GAIN 190 FEET
AVERAGE GRADIENT 3.9%
CLIMB
PROFILE .....ıllIlllll

0   500m

gradually steepening until it reaches the last of three white lines across the road. From here, the road bends to the right and the climbing subsides. A track peels off to the left after the road leaves its forest border to continue with its wide sweep to the right, now in open country.

A short, sharp climb lies ahead. You should find the start marked by the last set of hay bales on the left-hand side of the road. The ascent is straight and technically straightforward, but far from easy physically, topping out as the road bends to the right,

just beyond the third white line crossing the slope.

From this point, there is a slight downhill to enter the forest beyond. The road rises gently through a chicane (left, right, then sharp left), passing a distinct observation tower at the right-hand bend and finally emerging into open hillside. The top of the climb is reached just before the motorsport finish line across the road. From the summit, there are fine views across the Teith Valley toward the Gargunnock Hills that lie beyond.

THE DUKE'S PASS ABERFOYLE

Distance 2.6 miles/4.2km
Total Height Gain 745ft/227m
Altitude Range 69-804ft/21-245m
Average Gradient 5.4%
Start A821/B829 junction in Aberfoyle (NN 521010)
End Viewpoint at summit of Duke's Pass (NN 520037)
Map OS Landranger 57
Rail Balloch Station (18 miles), Stirling Station (19 miles)

Views tend to be obscured by the Queen Elizabeth Forest Park, but the true beauty of this route is to follow in the treads of generations of Scottish cyclists in summiting one of the country's most revered road hillclimbs.

Climb steeply away from the A821/B829 junction in Aberfoyle on a short straight, before sweeping to the right. A longer straight follows, with the gradient easing momentarily on passing the roadside steps at the village green. The incline steepens on the wide switchback to the left around the green to leave Aberfoyle behind and enter the forest.

A straight after the switchback precedes a chicane (right, then left) and two steeper switchbacks (right, then left). Road quality is much better through these, with forward vision improving as the road straightens beyond. The road flattens at the bends on approach to the entrance to the David Marshall Lodge Visitor Centre.

Rising again at the sharp bend to the right, the road continues through a wider arc to the right that brings it to the foot of a switchback. At the start of the left-hand turn, catch a glimpse of the Campsie Fells and Gargunnock Hills before the short straight that is a prelude to some sharp bends. Another straight beyond the bends leads to a false summit, with a slight dip on the far side and good views to the right. Stiff, steady climbing ensues as the road

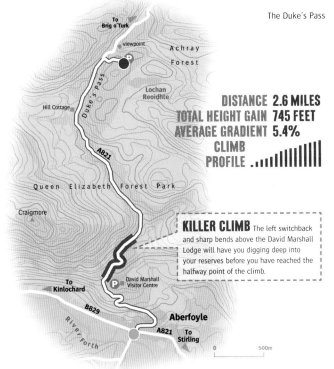

DISTANCE 2.6 MILES
TOTAL HEIGHT GAIN 745 FEET
AVERAGE GRADIENT 5.4%
CLIMB PROFILE

KILLER CLIMB The left switchback and sharp bends above the David Marshall Lodge will have you digging deep into your reserves before you have reached the halfway point of the climb.

sweeps to the left, turning more sharply at a footpath sign. Having changed direction, a lower summit is passed at the sign announcing this as Duke's Pass.

An imperceptible climb in open aspect comes next, with the forest set further back from the road. Parking places are passed and the road begins to rise away once more at a right-hand bend on approaching a bridge. A dip down from the bridge is followed by another stretch of imperceptible climbing. The road then starts

to twist and turn sharply, first with steeper climbing and then gentle.

Turn to the right at a sharp bend before the house for an abrupt climb. The incline eases on approach to a roadsign for the Three Lochs Forest Drive. After the parking area to the right, turn off into this forest. The road becomes much rougher after the first bend. A wide, sweeping bend to the right precedes a gentler curve to the left, after which the road climbs more steeply to summit at the vernacular stone signs.

STAT PAGE